Efficient R Programming
A Practical Guide to Smarter Programming

Colin Gillespie and Robin Lovelace

Beijing · Boston · Farnham · Sebastopol · Tokyo

Efficient R Programming

by Colin Gillespie and Robin Lovelace

Copyright © 2017 Colin Gillespie, Robin Lovelace. All rights reserved.

Printed in the United States of America.

Published by O'Reilly Media, Inc., 1005 Gravenstein Highway North, Sebastopol, CA 95472.

O'Reilly books may be purchased for educational, business, or sales promotional use. Online editions are also available for most titles (*http://oreilly.com/safari*). For more information, contact our corporate/institutional sales department: 800-998-9938 or *corporate@oreilly.com*.

Editor: Nicole Tache

Production Editor: Nicholas Adams

Copyeditor: Gillian McGarvey

Proofreader: Christina Edwards

Indexer: WordCo Indexing Services

Interior Designer: David Futato

Cover Designer: Randy Comer

Illustrator: Rebecca Demarest

December 2016:   First Edition

Revision History for the First Edition

2016-11-29:   First Release

See *http://oreilly.com/catalog/errata.csp?isbn=9781491950784* for release details.

978-1-491-95078-4

[LSI]

Table of Contents

Preface... ix

1. Introduction... 1
    Prerequisites   2
    Who This Book Is for and How to Use It   2
    What Is Efficiency?   4
    What Is Efficient R Programming?   4
    Why Efficiency?   6
    Cross-Transferable Skills for Efficiency   7
        Touch Typing   7
        Consistent Style and Code Conventions   8
    Benchmarking and Profiling   9
        Benchmarking   9
        Benchmarking Example   10
        Profiling   11
    Book Resources   14
        R Package   14
        Online Version   14
    References   14

2. Efficient Setup.. 17
    Prerequisites   18
    Top Five Tips for an Efficient R Setup   18
    Operating System   18
        Operating System and Resource Monitoring   19
    R Version   21
        Installing R   22
        Updating R   23

Installing R Packages   23
Installing R Packages with Dependencies   24
Updating R Packages   24
R Startup   25
R Startup Arguments   25
An Overview of R's Startup Files   26
The Location of Startup Files   27
The .Rprofile File   28
Example .Rprofile File   29
The .Renviron File   33
RStudio   35
Installing and Updating RStudio   35
Window Pane Layout   36
RStudio Options   38
Autocompletion   39
Keyboard Shortcuts   40
Object Display and Output Table   41
Project Management   41
BLAS and Alternative R Interpreters   43
Testing Performance Gains from BLAS   44
Other Interpreters   45
Useful BLAS/Benchmarking Resources   46
References   46

3. Efficient Programming. 47
Prerequisites   47
Top Five Tips for Efficient Programming   47
General Advice   48
Memory Allocation   49
Vectorized Code   50
Communicating with the User   53
Fatal Errors: stop()   53
Warnings: warning()   54
Informative Output: message() and cat()   55
Invisible Returns   55
Factors   56
Inherent Order   56
Fixed Set of Categories   57
The Apply Family   57
Example: Movies Dataset   59
Type Consistency   60
Caching Variables   61

Function Closures   63
The Byte Compiler   64
Example: The Mean Function   65
Compiling Code   66
References   67

4. Efficient Workflow.. 69
Prerequisites   69
Top Five Tips for Efficient Workflow   70
A Project Planning Typology   70
Project Planning and Management   72
Chunking Your Work   73
Making Your Workflow SMART   74
Visualizing Plans with R   75
Package Selection   76
Searching for R Packages   78
How to Select a Package   78
Publication   80
Dynamic Documents with R Markdown   81
R Packages   83
Reference   84

5. Efficient Input/Output....................................... 85
Prerequisites   86
Top Five Tips for Efficient Data I/O   86
Versatile Data Import with rio   86
Plain-Text Formats   88
Differences Between fread() and read_csv()   90
Preprocessing Text Outside R   92
Binary File Formats   93
Native Binary Formats: Rdata or Rds?   94
The Feather File Format   94
Benchmarking Binary File Formats   94
Protocol Buffers   96
Getting Data from the Internet   96
Accessing Data Stored in Packages   97
References   98

6. Efficient Data Carpentry..................................... 99
Prerequisites   100
Top Five Tips for Efficient Data Carpentry   100
Efficient Data Frames with tibble   100

Tidying Data with tidyr and Regular Expressions   102
    Make Wide Tables Long with gather()   103
    Split Joint Variables with separate()   104
    Other tidyr Functions   105
    Regular Expressions   106
Efficient Data Processing with dplyr   108
    Renaming Columns   110
    Changing Column Classes   110
    Filtering Rows   111
    Chaining Operations   112
    Data Aggregation   114
    Nonstandard Evaluation   117
Combining Datasets   118
Working with Databases   119
    Databases and dplyr   121
Data Processing with data.table   123
References   125

7. Efficient Optimization. 127
Prerequisites   128
Top Five Tips for Efficient Optimization   128
Code Profiling   128
    Getting Started with profvis   129
    Example: Monopoly Simulation   130
Efficient Base R   131
    The if() Versus ifelse() Functions   131
    Sorting and Ordering   132
    Reversing Elements   133
    Which Indices are TRUE?   133
    Converting Factors to Numerics   134
    Logical AND and OR   134
    Row and Column Operations   134
    is.na() and anyNA()   135
    Matrices   135
Example: Optimizing the move_square() Function   138
Parallel Computing   139
    Parallel Versions of Apply Functions   140
    Example: Snakes and Ladders   140
    Exit Functions with Care   141
    Parallel Code under Linux and OS X   141
Rcpp   142
    A Simple C++ Function   143

The cppFunction() Command   144
C++ Data Types   145
The sourceCpp() Function   145
Vectors and Loops   146
Matrices   149
C++ with Sugar on Top   149
Rcpp Resources   150
References   151

8. Efficient Hardware.. 153
Prerequisites   153
Top Five Tips for Efficient Hardware   153
Background: What Is a Byte?   154
Random Access Memory   155
Hard Drives: HDD Versus SSD   158
Operating Systems: 32-Bit or 64-Bit   159
Central Processing Unit   160
Cloud Computing   162
    Amazon EC2   162

9. Efficient Collaboration... 163
Prerequisites   164
Top Five Tips for Efficient Collaboration   164
Coding Style   164
    Reformatting Code with RStudio   165
    Filenames   165
    Loading Packages   166
    Commenting   166
    Object Names   167
    Example Package   167
    Assignment   168
    Spacing   168
    Indentation   168
    Curly Braces   169
Version Control   169
    Commits   170
    Git Integration in RStudio   170
    GitHub   171
    Branches, Forks, Pulls, and Clones   172
Code Review   173
References   174

10. Efficient Learning... 175

    Prerequisties   175
    Top Five Tips for Efficient Learning   175
    Using R's Internal Help   176
      Searching R for Topics   177
      Finding and Using Vignettes   178
      Getting Help on Functions   179
      Reading R Source Code   181
      swirl   182
    Online Resources   182
      Stack Overflow   183
      Mailing Lists and Groups   184
    Asking a Question   184
      Minimal Dataset   184
      Minimal Example   185
    Learning In Depth   185
    Spread the Knowledge   187
    References   187

A. Package Dependencies.. 189

B. References.. 191

Index... 197

Preface

Efficient R Programming is about increasing the amount of work you can do with R in a given amount of time. It's about both *computational* and *programmer* efficiency. There are many excellent R resources about topics such as visualization (e.g., Chang 2012), data science (e.g., Grolemund and Wickham 2016), and package development (e.g., Wickham 2015). There are even more resources on how to use R in particular domains, including Bayesian statistics, machine learning, and geographic information systems. However, there are very few unified resources on how to simply make R work effectively. Hints, tips, and decades of community knowledge on the subject are scattered across hundreds of internet pages, email threads, and discussion forums, making it challenging for R users to understand how to write efficient code.

In our teaching we have found that this issue applies to beginners and experienced users alike. Whether it's a question of understanding how to use R's vector objects to avoid for loops, knowing how to set up your *.Rprofile* and *.Renviron* files, or the ability to harness R's excellent C++ interface to do the heavy lifting, the concept of efficiency is key. The book aims to distill tips, warnings, and tricks of the trade into a single, cohesive whole that provides a useful resource to R programmers of all stripes for years to come.

The content of the book reflects the questions that our students from a range of disciplines, skill levels, and industries have asked over the years to make their R work faster. How to set up my system optimally for R programming work? How can one apply general principles from computer science (such as *do not repeat yourself*, aka DRY) to the specifics of an R script? How can R code be incorporated into an efficient workflow, including project inception, collaboration, and write-up? And how can one quickly learn how to use new packages and functions?

The book answers these questions and more in 10 self-contained chapters. Each chapter starts with the basics and gets progressively more advanced, so there is something for everyone in each one. While more advanced topics such as parallel programming and C++ may not be immediately relevant to R beginners, the book helps to navigate R's infamously steep learning curve with a commitment to starting slow and building on strong foundations. Thus even experienced R users are likely to find previously hidden gems of advice. While teaching this material, we commonly hear "Why didn't anyone tell me that before?"

Efficient programming should not be seen as an optional extra, and the importance of efficiency grows with the size of projects and datasets. In fact, this book was devised while teaching a course called *R for Big Data*, when it quickly became apparent that if you want to work with large datasets, your code must work efficiently. Even with small datasets, efficient code that is both fast to write and fast to run is a vital component of successful R projects. We found that the concept of efficient programming is important in all branches of the R community. Whether you are a sporadic user of R (e.g., for its unbeatable range of statistical packages), looking to develop a package, or working on a large collaborative project in which efficiency is mission-critical, code efficiency will have a major impact on your productivity.

Ultimately, efficiency is about getting more output for less work input. To take the analogy of a car, would you rather drive 1,000 km on a single tank (or a single charge of batteries) or refuel a heavy, clunky, ugly car every 50 km? Or would you prefer to choose an altogether more efficient vehicle and cycle? In the same way, efficient R code is better than inefficient R code in almost every way: it is easier to read, write, run, share, and maintain. This book cannot provide all the answers about how to produce such code, but it certainly can provide ideas, example code, and tips to make a start in the right direction of travel.

Conventions Used in This Book

The following typographical conventions are used in this book:

Italic
> Indicates new terms, URLs, email addresses, filenames, and file extensions.

Bold
> Indicates the names of R packages.

`Constant width`
> Used for program listings, as well as within paragraphs to refer to program elements such as variable or function names, databases, data types, environment variables, statements, and keywords.

`Constant width bold`
> Shows commands or other text that should be typed literally by the user.

`Constant width italic`

Shows text that should be replaced with user-supplied values or by values determined by context.

This element signifies a tip or suggestion.

This element signifies a general note.

This element indicates a warning or caution.

Using Code Examples

Supplemental material (code examples, exercises, etc.) is available for download at *https://github.com/csgillespie/efficient*.

This book is here to help you get your job done. In general, if example code is offered with this book, you may use it in your programs and documentation. You do not need to contact us for permission unless you're reproducing a significant portion of the code. For example, writing a program that uses several chunks of code from this book does not require permission. Selling or distributing a CD-ROM of examples from O'Reilly books does require permission. Answering a question by citing this book and quoting example code does not require permission. Incorporating a significant amount of example code from this book into your product's documentation does require permission.

We appreciate, but do not require, attribution. An attribution usually includes the title, author, publisher, and ISBN. For example: "*Efficient R Programming* by Colin Gillespie and Robin Lovelace (O'Reilly). Copyright 2017 Colin Gillespie, Robin Lovelace, 978-1-491-95078-4."

If you feel your use of code examples falls outside fair use or the permission given above, feel free to contact us at *permissions@oreilly.com*.

O'Reilly Safari

Safari (formerly Safari Books Online) is a membership-based training and reference platform for enterprise, government, educators, and individuals.

Members have access to thousands of books, training videos, Learning Paths, interactive tutorials, and curated playlists from over 250 publishers, including O'Reilly Media, Harvard Business Review, Prentice Hall Professional, Addison-Wesley Professional, Microsoft Press, Sams, Que, Peachpit Press, Adobe, Focal Press, Cisco Press, John Wiley & Sons, Syngress, Morgan Kaufmann, IBM Redbooks, Packt, Adobe Press, FT Press, Apress, Manning, New Riders, McGraw-Hill, Jones & Bartlett, and Course Technology, among others.

For more information, please visit *http://oreilly.com/safari*.

How to Contact Us

Please address comments and questions concerning this book to the publisher:

> O'Reilly Media, Inc.
> 1005 Gravenstein Highway North
> Sebastopol, CA 95472
> 800-998-9938 (in the United States or Canada)
> 707-829-0515 (international or local)
> 707-829-0104 (fax)

We have a web page for this book, where we list errata, examples, and any additional information. You can access this page at *http://bit.ly/efficient-r-programming*.

To comment or ask technical questions about this book, send email to *bookquestions@oreilly.com*.

For more information about our books, courses, conferences, and news, see our website at *http://www.oreilly.com*.

Find us on Facebook: *http://facebook.com/oreilly*

Follow us on Twitter: *http://twitter.com/oreillymedia*

Watch us on YouTube: *http://www.youtube.com/oreillymedia*

Acknowledgments

This book was written in the open, and many people contributed pull requests to fix minor problems. Special thanks goes to O'Reilly who allowed this process and everyone who contributed via GitHub: @Delvis, @richelbilderbeek, @adamryczkowski,

@CSJCampbell, @tktan, @nachti, Conor Lawless, @timcdlucas, Dirk Eddelbuettel, @wolfganglederer, @HenrikBengtsson, @giocomai, and @daattali.

Many thanks also to the detailed feedback from the technical reviewers, Richard Cotton and Garrett Grolemund.

Colin

To Esther, Nathan, and Niamh. Thanks for your patience.

Robin

Thanks to my housemates in Cornerstone Housing Cooperative for putting up with me being antisocial while in *book mode*. To everyone at the University of Leeds for encouraging me to pursue projects outside the usual academic pursuits of journal articles and conferences. And thanks to everyone involved in the community of open source developers, users, and communicators who made all this possible.

## CHAPTER 1

Introduction

This chapter describes the wide range of people this book was written for, in terms of R and programming experience, and how you can get the most out of it. Anyone setting out to improve efficiency should have an understanding of precisely what they mean by the term, and this is discussed with reference to *algorithmic* and *programmer* efficiency in "What Is Efficiency?" on page 4, and with reference to R in particular in "What Is Efficient R Programming?" on the same page. It may seem obvious, but it's also worth thinking about *why* anyone would bother with efficient code now that powerful computers are cheap and accessible. This is covered in "Why Efficiency?" on page 6.

This book happily is not completely R-specific. Non R–programming skills that are needed for efficient R programming, which you will develop during the course of following this book, are covered in "Cross-Transferable Skills for Efficiency" on page 7. Atypically for a book about programming, this section introduces touch typing and consistency, cross-transferable skills that should improve your efficiency beyond programming. However, this is first and foremost a book about programming and it wouldn't be so without code examples in every chapter. Despite being more conceptual and discursive, this opening chapter is no exception: its penultimate section ("Benchmarking and Profiling" on page 9) describes two essential tools in the efficient R programmer's toolbox and how to use them with a couple of illustrative examples. The final thing to say at the outset is how to use this book in conjunction with the book's associated package and its source code. This is covered in "Book Resources" on page 14.

Prerequisites

As emphasized in the next section, it's useful to run code and experiment as you read. This section, found at the beginning of each chapter, ensures that you have the necessary packages for each chapter. The prerequisites for this chapter are:

- A working installation of R on your computer (see "Installing and Updating RStudio" on page 35).
- Install and load the **microbenchmark**, **profvis**, and **ggplot2** packages (see "Installing R Packages" on page 23 for tips on installing packages and keeping them up-to-date). You can ensure that these packages are installed by loading them as follows:

```
library("microbenchmark")
library("profvis")
library("ggplot2")
```

The prerequisites needed to run the code contained in the entire book are covered in "Book Resources" on page 14 at the end of this chapter.

Who This Book Is for and How to Use It

This book is for anyone who wants to make their R code faster to type, faster to run, and more scalable. These considerations generally come *after* learning the very basics of R for data analysis; we assume you are either accustomed to R or proficient at programming in other languages, although this book could still be of use for beginners. Thus the book should be useful to people with a range of skill levels, who can broadly be divided into three groups:

For programmers with little experience with R
> This book will help you navigate the quirks of R to make it work efficiently: it is easy to write slow R code if you treat it as if it were another language.

For R users with little experience in programming
> This book will show you many concepts and tricks of the trade, some of which are borrowed from computer science, that will make your work more time effective.

For R beginners with little experience in programming
> This book can steer you to get things right (or at least less wrong) at the outset. Bad habits are easy to gain but hard to lose. Reading this book at the outset of your programming career could save you many hours in the future searching the web for issues covered in this book.

Identifying which group you best fit into will help you get the most out of it. For everyone, we recommend reading *Efficient R Programming* while you have an active R project on the go, whether it's a collaborative task at work or simply a personal project at home. Why? The scope of this book is wider than most programming textbooks (Chapter 4 covers project management, for example) and working on a project outside the confines of it will help put the concepts, recommendations, and code into practice. Going directly from words into action in this way will help ensure that the information is consolidated: learn by doing.

If you're an R novice and fit into the final category, we recommend that this active R project not be an important deliverable, but another R resource. Though this book is generic, it is likely that your usage of R will be largely domain-specific. For this reason, we recommend reading it alongside teaching material in your chosen area. Furthermore, we advocate that all readers use this book alongside other R resources such as the numerous vignettes, tutorials, and online articles that the R community has produced (described in the following tip). At a bare minimum, you should be familiar with data frames, looping, and simple plots, which you will learn from these resources.

Resources for Learning R

There are many places to find generic and domain-specific R teaching materials. For complete beginners, there are a number of introductory resources, such as the excellent Student's Guide to R (*http://bit.ly/studentguider*) and the more technical IcebreakeR (*http://bit.ly/icebreakR*) tutorial.

R also comes preinstalled with guidance, revealed by entering `help.start()` into the R console, including the classic official guide *An Introduction to R*, which is excellent, but daunting to many. Entering `vignette()` will display a list of guides packaged *within your R installation* (and hence do not require an internet connection). To see the vignette for a specific topic, just enter the vignette's name into the same command (e.g., `vignette(package = "dplyr", "introduction")`) to see the introductory vignette for the `dplyr` package.

Another early port of call should be the Comprehensive R Archive Network (CRAN) (*https://cran.r-project.org/index.html*) website. The Contributed Documentation (*https://cran.r-project.org/other-docs.html*) page contains a list of contributed resources, mainly tutorials, on subjects ranging from map making (*http://bit.ly/mapsinR*) to econometrics (*http://bit.ly/econometricR*). The new bookdown website (*https://bookdown.org/*) contains a list of complete (or near complete) books that cover domains such as *R for Data Science* (*http://r4ds.had.co.nz/*) and Authoring Books with R Markdown (*https://bookdown.org/yihui/bookdown/*). We recommend keeping your eye on the *R-o-sphere* via the R-Bloggers (*http://r-bloggers.com/*) website, popular Twitter

---

feeds, and CRAN-affiliated email lists (*https://www.r-project.org/mail.html*) for up-to-date materials that can be used in conjunction with this book.

What Is Efficiency?

In everyday life, efficiency roughly means *working well*. An efficient vehicle goes far without guzzling gas. An efficient worker gets the job done fast without stress. And an efficient light shines brightly with a minimum of energy consumption. In this final sense, efficiency (η) has a formal definition as the ratio of work done (W, light output) per unit effort (Q, energy consumption in this case):

$$\eta = \frac{W}{Q}$$

How does this translate into programming? Efficient code can be defined narrowly or broadly. The first, more narrow definition is *algorithmic efficiency*: how fast the computer can undertake a piece of work given a particular piece of code. This concept dates back to the very origins of computing, as illustrated by the following quote by Ada Lovelace (1842) in her notes on the work of Charles Babbage:

> In almost every computation a great variety of arrangements for the succession of the processes is possible, and various considerations must influence the selections amongst them for the purposes of a calculating engine. One essential object is to choose that arrangement which shall tend to reduce to a minimum the time necessary for completing the calculation.

The second, broader definition of efficient computing is *programmer productivity*. This is the amount of useful work a person (not a computer) can do per unit time. It may be possible to rewrite your code base in C to make it 100 times faster. But if this takes 100 human hours, it may not be worth it. Computers can chug away day and night. People cannot. Human productivity is the subject of Chapter 4.

By the end of this book, you should know how to write code that is efficient from both *algorithmic* and *productivity* perspectives. Efficient code is also concise, elegant, and easy to maintain, which is vital when working on large projects. But this raises the wider question: what is different about efficient R code compared with efficient code in any other language?

What Is Efficient R Programming?

The issue flagged by Ada of having a *great variety* of ways to solve a problem is key to understanding how efficient R programming differs from efficient programming in other languages. R is notorious for allowing users to solve problems in many ways. This is due to R's inherent flexibility, in which almost "anything can be modified after it is created" (Wickham 2014). R's inventors, Ross Ihaka and Robert Gentleman, designed it to be this way: a cell in a data frame can be selected in multiple ways in base R alone (three of which are illustrated later in this chapter, in "Benchmarking Example" on page 10). This is useful because it allows programmers to use the language as best suits their needs, but it can be confusing for people looking for the *right* way of doing things and can cause inefficiencies if you don't fully understand the language.

R's notoriety for being able to solve a problem in multiple ways has grown with the proliferation of community-contributed packages. In this book, we focus on the best way of solving problems from an efficiency perspective. Often it is instructive to discover why a certain way of doing things is faster than other ways. However, if your aim is simply to *get stuff done*, you only need to know what is likely to be the most efficient way. In this way, R's flexibility can be inefficient: although it may be easier to find *a* way of solving any given problem in R than other languages, solving the problem with R may make it harder to find *the best* way to solve that problem, as there are so many. This book tackles this issue head on by recommending what we believe are the most efficient approaches. We hope you trust our views, based on years of using and teaching R, but we also hope that you challenge them at times and test them with benchmarks if you suspect there's a better way of doing things (thanks to R's flexibility and ability to interface with other languages, there may well be).

It is well known that R code can lack algorithmic efficiency compared with low-level languages for certain tasks, especially if it was written by someone who doesn't fully understand the language. But it is worth highlighting the numerous ways that R encourages and guides efficiency, especially programmer efficiency:

- R is not compiled, but it calls compiled code. This means that you get the best of both worlds: thankfully, R removes the laborious stage of compiling your code before being able to run it, but provides impressive speed gains by calling compiled C, FORTRAN, and other language behind the scenes.

- R is a functional and object-orientated language (Wickham 2014). This means that it is possible to write complex and flexible functions in R that get a huge amount of work done with a single line of code.

- R uses RAM for memory. This may seem obvious, but it's worth saying: RAM is much faster than any hard disk system. Compared with databases, R is therefore very fast at common data manipulation, processing, and modeling operations. RAM is now cheaper than ever, meaning the potential downsides of this feature are further away than ever.

- R is supported by excellent integrated development environments (IDEs). The environment in which you program can have a huge impact on programmer efficiency as it can provide help quickly, allow for interactive plotting, and allow your R projects to be tightly integrated with other aspects of your project such as file management, version management, and interactive visualization systems, as discussed in "RStudio" on page 35.

- R has a strong user community. This boosts efficiency because if you encounter a problem that has not yet been solved, you can simply ask the community. If it is a new, clearly stated, and reproducible question asked on a popular forum such as Stack Overflow (*https://stackoverflow.com/*) or an appropriate R list (*https://www.r-project.org/mail.html*), you are likely to get a response from an accomplished R programmer within minutes. The obvious benefit of this crowd-sourced support system is that the efficiency benefits of the answer will, from that moment on, be available to everyone.

Efficient R programming is the implementation of efficient programming practices in R. All languages are different, so efficient R code does not look like efficient code in another language. Many packages have been optimized for performance so, for some operations, achieving maximum computational efficiency may simply be a case of selecting the appropriate package and using it correctly. There are many ways to get the same result in R, and some are very slow. Therefore, *not* writing slow code should be prioritized over writing fast code.

Returning to the analogy of the two cars sketched in the preface, efficient R programming for some use cases can simply mean trading in your old, heavy, gas-guzzling SUV function for a lightweight velomobile. The search for optimal performance often has diminishing returns, so it is important to find bottlenecks in your code to prioritize work for maximum increases in computational efficiency. Linking back to R's notoriety as a flexible language, efficient R programming can be interpreted as finding a solution that is fast enough in terms of computational efficiency but as fast as possible in terms of programmer efficiency. After all, you and your coworkers probably have better and more valuable things to do outside work, so it is important that you get the job done quickly and take time off for other interesting pursuits.

Why Efficiency?

Computers are always getting more powerful. Does this not reduce the need for efficient computing? The answer is simple: no. In an age of Big Data and stagnating computer clock speeds (see Chapter 8), computational bottlenecks are more likely than ever before to hamper your work. An efficient programmer can "solve more complex tasks, ask more ambitious questions, and include more sophisticated analyses in their research" (Visser et al. 2015).

A concrete example illustrates the importance of efficiency in mission-critical situations. Robin was working on a tight contract for the UK's Department for Transport to build the Propensity to Cycle Tool, an online application that had to be ready for national deployment in less than four months. For this work, he developed the function line2route() in the **stplanr** package to generate routes via the (CycleStreets (*http://www.cyclestreets.net/*)) API. Hundreds of thousands of routes were needed, but, to his dismay, code slowed to a standstill after only a few thousand routes. This endangered the contract. After eliminating other issues and via code profiling (covered in "Code Profiling" on page 128), it was found that the slowdown was due to a bug in line2route(): it suffered from the *vector growing problem*, discussed in "Memory Allocation" on page 49.

The solution was simple. A single commit (*http://bit.ly/refactorline2route*) made line2route() more than ten times faster and substantially shorter. This potentially saved the project from failure. The moral of this story is that efficient programming is not merely a desirable skill—it can be essential.

There are many concepts and skills that are language-agnostic. Much of the knowledge imparted in this book should be relevant to programming in other languages (and other technical activities beyond programming). There are strong reasons for focusing on efficiency in one language, however. In R, simply using replacement functions from a different package can greatly improve efficiency, as discussed in relation to reading text files in Chapter 5. This level of detail, with reproducible examples, would not be possible in a general-purpose efficient programming book. Skills for efficient working, which apply beyond R programming, are covered in the next section.

Cross-Transferable Skills for Efficiency

The meaning of *efficient R code*, as opposed to generic *efficient code*, should be clear from reading the preceding two sections. However, that does not mean that the skills and concepts covered in this book are not transferable to other languages and non-programming tasks. Likewise, working on these cross-transferable skills will improve your R programming (as well as other aspects of your working life). Two of these skills are especially important: touch typing and use of a consistent style.

Touch Typing

The other side of the efficiency coin is programmer efficiency. There are many things that will help increase the productivity of you and your collaborators, not least following the advice of Philipp Janert to "think more, work less" (Janert 2010). The evidence suggests that good diet, physical activity, plenty of sleep, and a healthy work-life balance can all boost your speed and effectiveness at work (Jensen 2011; Pereira et al. 2015; Grant, Spurgeon, and Wallace 2013).

While we recommend that the reader reflect on this evidence and their own well-being, this is not a self-help book. It is a book about programming. However, there is one nonprogramming skill that *can* have a huge impact on productivity: touch typing. This skill can be relatively painless to learn, and can have a huge impact on your ability to write, modify, and test R code quickly. Learning to touch type properly will pay off in small increments throughout the rest of your programming life (of course, the benefits are not constrained to R programming).

The key difference between a touch typist and someone who constantly looks down at the keyboard, or who uses only two or three fingers for typing, is hand placement. Touch typing involves positioning your hands on the keyboard with each finger of both hands touching or hovering over a specific letter (Figure 1-1). This takes time and some discipline to learn. Fortunately there are many resources that will help you get in the habit early, including the open source software projects Klavaro (*https:// sourceforge.net/projects/klavaro/*) and TypeFaster (*https://sourceforge.net/projects/type faster/*).

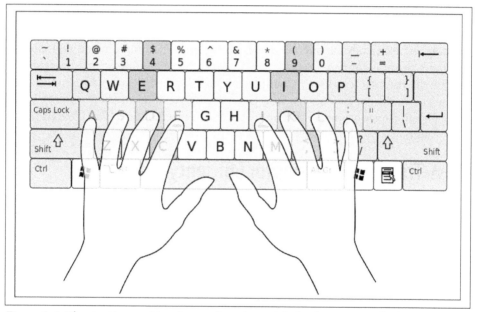

Figure 1-1. The starting position for touch typing, with the fingers over the home keys. Source: Wikipedia (https://commons.wikimedia.org/wiki/File:QWERTY-home-keys-position.svg) under the Creative Commons license.

Consistent Style and Code Conventions

Getting into the habit of clear and consistent style when writing anything, be it code or poetry, will have benefits in many other projects, programming or non-programming. As outlined in "Coding Style" on page 164, style is to some extent a personal preference. However, it is worth noting the conventions we use at the outset of this book, to maximize its readability. Throughout this book we use a consistent set of conventions to refer to code.

- Package names are in bold, e.g., **dplyr**.

- Functions are in a code font, followed by parentheses, like `plot()` or `median()`.

- Other R objects, such as data or function arguments, are in a code font without parentheses, like `x` and `name`.

- Occasionally, we'll highlight the package of the function using two colons, like `microbenchmark::microbenchmark()`. Note that this notation can be efficient if you only need to use a package's function once, as it avoids attaching the package.

The concepts of benchmarking and profiling are not R-specific. However, they are done in a particular way in R, as outlined in the next section.

Benchmarking and Profiling

Benchmarking and profiling are key to efficient programming, especially in R. Benchmarking is the process of testing the performance of specific operations repeatedly. Profiling involves running many lines of code to find bottlenecks. Both are vital for understanding efficiency, and we use them throughout the book. Their centrality to efficient programming practice means they must be covered in this introductory chapter, despite being seen by many as an intermediate or advanced R programming topic.

In some ways, benchmarks can be seen as the building blocks of profiles. Profiling can be understood as automatically running many benchmarks for every line in a script and comparing the results line by line. Because benchmarks are smaller, easier, and more modular, we cover them first.

Benchmarking

Modifying elements from one benchmark to the next and recording the results after the modification enables us to determine the fastest piece of code. Benchmarking is important in the efficient programmer's toolkit: you may *think* that your code is faster than mine, but benchmarking allows you to *prove* it. The easiest way to benchmark a function is to use `system.time()`. However, it is important to remember that we are taking a sample. We wouldn't expect a single person in London to be representative of the entire UK population; similarly, a single benchmark provides us with a single observation on our function's behavior. Therefore, we'll need to repeat the timing many times with a loop.

An alternative way of benchmarking is via the flexible **microbenchmark** package. This allows us to easily run each function multiple times (by default, 100) in order to detect microsecond differences in code performance. We then get a convenient summary of the results: the minimum/maximum and lower/upper quartiles, and the mean/median times. We suggest focusing on the median time to get a feel for the standard time and the quartiles to understand the variability.

Benchmarking Example

A good example is testing different methods to look up a single value in a data frame. Note that each argument in the following benchmark is a term to be evaluated (for multi-line benchmarks, the term to be evaluated can be surrounded by curly brackets, {}).

```
library("microbenchmark")
df = data.frame(v = 1:4, name = letters[1:4])
microbenchmark(df[3, 2], df[3, "name"], df$name[3])
# Unit: microseconds
#           expr    min    lq  mean median    uq   max neval cld
#       df[3, 2]  17.99 18.96 20.16  19.38 19.77 35.14   100   b
# df[3, "name"]  17.97 19.13 21.45  19.64 20.15 74.00   100   b
#     df$name[3]  12.48 13.81 15.81  14.48 15.14 67.24   100   a
```

The results summarize how long each query took: the minimum (min); lower and upper quartiles (lq and uq, respectively); and the mean, median, and maximum (max) for each of the number of evaluations (neval, with the default value of 100 used in this case). cld reports the relative rank of each row in the form of *compact letter display*: in this case, df$name[3] performs best, with a rank of a and a mean time of around 25% lower than the other two functions.

When using microbenchmark(), you should pay careful attention to the units. In the previous example, each function call takes approximately 20 *microseconds*, implying around 50,000 function calls could be done in a second. When comparing quick functions, the standard units are:

milliseconds (ms)
    One thousand functions takes a second;

microseconds (μs)
    one million function calls takes a second;

nanoseconds (ns)
    one billion calls takes a second.

We can set the units we want to use with the unit argument (e.g., the results are reported in seconds if we set unit = "s").

When thinking about computational efficiency, there are (at least) two in measures:

Relative time
    df$name[3] is 25% faster than df[3, "name"];

Absolute time
df$name[3] is five microseconds faster than df[3, "name"].

Both measures are useful, but it is important not to forget the underlying time scale. It makes little sense to optimize a function that takes *microseconds* if there are operations that take *seconds* to complete in your code.

Profiling

Benchmarking generally tests the execution time of one function against another. Profiling, on the other hand, is about testing large chunks of code.

It is difficult to overemphasize the importance of profiling for efficient R programming. Without a profile of what took longest, you will have only a vague idea of why your code is taking so long to run. The following example (which generates Figure 1-2, an image of ice-sheet retreat from 1985 to 2015) shows how profiling can be used to identify bottlenecks in your R scripts:

```
library("profvis")
profvis(expr = {

  # Stage 1: load packages
  # library("rnoaa") # not necessary as data pre-saved
  library("ggplot2")

  # Stage 2: load and process data
  out = readRDS("extdata/out-ice.Rds")
  df = dplyr::rbind_all(out, id = "Year")

  # Stage 3: visualize output
  ggplot(df, aes(long, lat, group = paste(group, Year))) +
    geom_path(aes(colour = Year))
  ggsave("figures/icesheet-test.png")
}, interval = 0.01, prof_output = "ice-prof")
```

The results of this profiling exercise are displayed in Figure 1-3.

For more information about profiling and benchmarking, please refer to the Optimising code (*http://adv-r.had.co.nz/Profiling.html*) chapter in *Advanced R* by Hadley Wickham (CRC Press), and "Code Profiling" on page 128 in this book. We recommend reading these additional resources while performing benchmarks and profiles on your own code, perhaps based on the following exercises.

Figure 1-2. Visualization of North Pole ice-sheet decline, generated using the code profiled using the profvis package

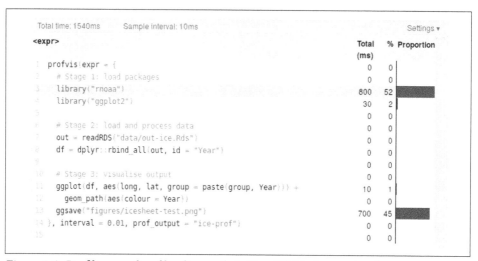

Figure 1-3. Profiling results of loading and plotting NASA data on ice-sheet retreat

Exercises

Consider the following benchmark to evaluate different functions for calculating the cumulative sum of all the whole numbers from 1 to 100:

```
x = 1:100 # initiate vector to cumulatively sum

# Method 1: with a for loop (10 lines)
```

```
cs_for = function(x){
  for(i in x){
    if(i == 1){
      xc = x[i]
    } else {
      xc = c(xc, sum(x[1:i]))
    }
  }
  xc
}

# Method 2: with apply (3 lines)
cs_apply = function(x){
  sapply(x, function(x) sum(1:x))
}

# Method 3: cumsum (1 line, not shown)
microbenchmark(cs_for(x), cs_apply(x), cumsum(x))
#> Unit: nanoseconds
#>         expr    min     lq   mean median     uq    max neval
#>    cs_for(x) 248145 316292 386893 370505 436382 697258   100
#>  cs_apply(x) 157610 198157 255241 233324 306013 478394   100
#>    cumsum(x)    561   1131   1796   1422   2075  18284   100
```

1. Which method is fastest and how many times faster is it?

2. Run the same benchmark, but with the results reported in seconds, on a vector of all the whole numbers from 1 to 50,000. Hint: also use the argument neval = 1 so that each command is only run once to ensure that the results complete (even with a single evaluation, the benchmark may take up to or more than a minute to complete, depending on your system). Does the *relative* time difference increase or decrease? By how much?

3. Test how long the different methods for subsetting the data frame df, presented in "Benchmarking Example" on page 10, take on your computer. Is it faster or slower at subsetting than the computer on which this book was compiled?

4. Use system.time() and a for() loop to test how long it takes to perform the subsetting operation 50,000 times. Before testing this, do you think it will be more or less than one second for each subsetting method? Hint: the test for the first method is shown in the following code:

```
# Test how long it takes to subset the data frame 50,000 times:
system.time(
  for(i in 1:50000) {
    df[3, 2]
  }
)
```

5. Bonus exercise: try profiling a section of code you have written using **profvis**. Where are the bottlenecks? Were they where you expected?

Book Resources

R Package

This book has an associated R package that contains datasets and functions referenced in the book. The package is hosted on GitHub (*https://github.com/csgillespie/efficient*) and can be installed using the **devtools** package:

```
devtools::install_github("csgillespie/efficient")
```

The package also contains solutions (as vignettes) to the exercises found in this book. They can be browsed with the following command:

```
browseVignettes(package = "efficient")
```

The following command will install all packages used to generate this book:

```
devtools::install_github("csgillespie/efficientR")
```

Online Version

We are grateful to O'Reilly for allowing us to develop this book online (*https://csgilles pie.github.io/efficientR/*). The online version constitutes a substantial additional resource to supplement this book, and will continue to evolve in between reprints of the physical book. The book's code also represents a substantial learning opportunity in itself as it was written using R Markdown and the **bookdown** package, allowing us to run the R code each time we compile the book to ensure that it works, and allowing others to contribute to its longevity. To edit this chapter, for example, simply navigate to *https://github.com/csgillespie/efficientR/edit/master/01-introduction.Rmd* while logged into a GitHub account (*http://bit.ly/newgithub*). The full source of the book is available at *https://github.com/csgillespie/efficientR* where we welcome comments/ questions on the Issue Tracker (*https://github.com/csgillespie/efficientR/issues*) and Pull Requests.

References

Wickham, Hadley. 2014a. *Advanced R*. CRC Press.

Visser, Marco D., Sean M. McMahon, Cory Merow, Philip M. Dixon, Sydne Record, and Eelke Jongejans. 2015. "Speeding Up Ecological and Evolutionary Computations in R; Essentials of High Performance Computing for Biologists." Edited by Francis

Ouellette. *PLOS Computational Biology* 11 (3): e1004140. doi:10.1371/journal.pcbi. 1004140 (*http://bit.ly/speedupR*).

Janert, Philipp K. 2010. *Data Analysis with Open Source Tools*. O'Reilly Media.

Jensen, Jørgen Dejgård. 2011. "Can Worksite Nutritional Interventions Improve Productivity and Firm Profitability? A Literature Review." *Perspectives in Public Health* 131 (4). SAGE Publications: 184–92.

Pereira, Michelle Jessica, Brooke Kaye Coombes, Tracy Anne Comans, and Venerina Johnston. 2015. "The Impact of Onsite Workplace Health-Enhancing Physical Activity Interventions on Worker Productivity: A Systematic Review." *Occupational and Environmental Medicine* 72 (6). BMJ Publishing Group Ltd: 401–12.

Grant, Christine A, Louise M Wallace, and Peter C Spurgeon. 2013. "An Exploration of the Psychological Factors Affecting Remote E-Worker's Job Effectiveness, Well-Being and Work-Life Balance." *Employee Relations* 35 (5). Emerald Group Publishing Limited: 527–46.

## CHAPTER 2

Efficient Setup

An efficient computer setup is analogous to a well-tuned vehicle. Its components work in harmony. It is well serviced. It's fast!

This chapter describes the setup that will enable a productive workflow. It explores how the operating system, R version, startup files, and IDE can make your R work faster. Understanding and at times changing these setup options can have many additional benefits. That's why we cover them at this early stage (hardware is covered in Chapter 3). By the end of this chapter, you should understand how to set up your computer and R installation for optimal efficiency. It covers the following topics:

R and the operating systems
> System monitoring on Linux, Mac, and Windows

R version
> How to keep your base R installation and packages up-to-date

R start-up
> How and why to adjust your *.Rprofile* and *.Renviron* files

RStudio
> An IDE to boost your programming productivity

BLAS and alternative R interpreters
> Looks at ways to make R faster

Efficient programming is more than a series of tips: there is no substitute for in-depth understanding. However, to help remember the key messages buried among the details, each chapter from now on contains a Top Five Tips section after the prerequisites.

Prerequisites

Only one package needs to be installed to run the code in this chapter:

```
library("benchmarkme")
```

Top Five Tips for an Efficient R Setup

1. Use system monitoring to identify bottlenecks in your hardware/code.

2. Keep your R installation and packages up-to-date.

3. Make use of RStudio's powerful autocompletion capabilities and shortcuts.

4. Store API keys in the *.Renviron* file.

5. Consider changing your BLAS library.

Operating System

R supports all three major operating system (OS) types: Linux, Mac, and Windows.[1] R is platform-independent, although there are some OS-specific quirks, such as in relation to file-path notation (see "The Location of Startup Files" on page 27).

Basic OS-specific information can be queried from within R using Sys.info():

```
Sys.info()
#> sysname    release              machine     user
#> "Linux"    "4.2.0-35-generic"   "x86_64"    "robin"
```

Translated into English, the preceding output means that R is running on a 64-bit (x86_64) Linux distribution (4.2.0-35-generic is the Linux version) and that the current user is robin. Four other pieces of information (not shown) are also produced by the command, the meaning of which is well documented in a help file revealed by entering ?Sys.info in the R console.

---

1 All CRAN packages are automatically tested on these systems, in addition to Solaris. R has also been reported to run on more exotic operating systems, including those used in smartphones and game consoles (Peng 2014).

The **assertive.reflection** package can be used to report additional information about your computer's operating system and R setup with functions for asserting operating system and other system characteristics. The `assert_*()` functions work by testing the truth of the statement and erroring if the statement is untrue. On a Linux system `assert_is_linux()` will run silently, whereas `assert_is_windows()` will cause an error. The package can also test for the IDE you are using (e.g., `assert_is_rstudio()`), the capabilities of R (`assert_r_has_libcurl_capability()`, etc.), and what OS tools are available (e.g., `assert_r_can_compile_code()`). These functions can be useful for running code that is designed only to run on one type of setup.

Operating System and Resource Monitoring

Minor differences aside, R's computational efficiency is broadly the same across different operating systems.[2] Beyond the 32-bit versus 64-bit issue (covered in Chapter 3) and *process forking* (covered in Chapter 7) another OS-related issue to consider is external dependencies: programs that R packages depend on. Sometimes external package dependencies must be installed manually (i.e., not using `install.pack ages()`). This is especially common on Unix-based systems (Linux and Mac). On Debian-based operating systems such as Ubuntu, many R packages can be installed at the OS level to ensure that external dependencies are also installed (see "Installing R Packages with Dependencies" on page 24).

Resource monitoring is the process of checking the status of key OS variables. For computationally intensive work, it is sensible to monitor system resources in this way. Resource monitoring can help identify computational bottlenecks. Alongside R profiling functions such as **profvis** (see "Code Profiling" on page 128), system monitoring provides a useful tool for understanding how R is performing in relation to variables reporting the OS state, such as how much RAM is in use, which relates to the wider question of whether more is needed (covered in Chapter 3).

CPU resources allocated over time is another common OS variable that is worth monitoring. A basic use case is to check whether your code is running in parallel (see

---

2 Benchmarking conducted for the presentation "R on Different Platforms" at useR! 2006 found that R was marginally faster on Windows than on Linux setups. Similar results were reported in an academic paper, with R completing statistical analyses faster on a Linux than on a Mac (Sekhon 2006). In 2015 Revolution R (*http://bit.ly/benchmarkRRO*) supported these results with slightly faster run times for certain benchmarks on Ubuntu than Mac systems. The data from the **benchmarkme** package also suggests that running code under the Linux OS is marginally faster.

Figure 2-1), and whether there is spare CPU capacity on the OS that could be harnessed by parallel code.

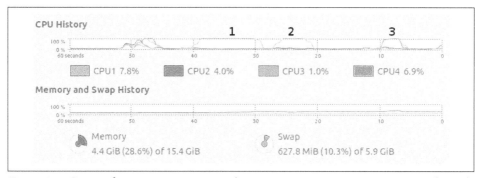

Figure 2-1. Output from a system monitor (gnome-system-monitor running on Ubuntu) showing the resources consumed by running the code presented in the second of the Exercises at the end of this section. The first increases RAM use, the second is single-threaded, and the third is multithreaded.

System monitoring is a complex topic that spills over into system administration and server management. Fortunately, there are many tools designed to ease monitoring on all major operating systems.

- On Linux, the shell command `top` displays key resource use figures for most distributions. `htop` and Gnome's System Monitor (`gnome-system-monitor`; see Figure 2-1) are more refined alternatives, which use command-line and graphical user interfaces, respectively. A number of options, such as `nethogs`, monitor internet usage.

- On Mac, the Activity Monitor provides similar functionality. This can be initiated from the Utilities folder in Launchpad.

- On Windows, the Task Manager provides key information on RAM and CPU use by process. This can be started in modern Windows versions by pressing Ctrl-Alt-Del or by clicking the taskbar and Start Task Manager.

Exercises

1. What is the exact version of your computer's operating system?

2. Start an activity monitor, then execute the following code chunk. In it, `lapply()` (or its parallel version, `mclapply()`) is used to apply the function `median()` over every column in the data frame object X (see "The Apply Family" on page 57 for more on the apply family of functions). The reason this works is that a data frame

is really a list of vectors, with each vector forming a column. How do the system output log results on your system compare to those presented in Figure 2-1?

```
# Note: uses 2+ GB RAM and takes several seconds depending on hardware
# 1: Create large dataset
X = as.data.frame(matrix(rnorm(1e8), nrow = 1e7))
# 2: Find the median of each column using a single core
r1 = lapply(X, median)
# 3: Find the median of each column using many cores
r2 = parallel::mclapply(X, median)
```

mclapply only works in parallel on Mac and Linux. In Chapter 7 you'll learn about the equivalent function parLapply() that works in parallel on Windows.

3. What do you notice regarding CPU usage, RAM, and system time during and after each of the three operations?

4. Bonus question: how would the results change depending on operating system?

R Version

It is important to be aware that R is an evolving software project, whose behavior changes over time. In general, base R is very conservative about making changes that break backwards compatibility. However, packages occasionally change substantially from one release to the next; typically it depends on the age of the package. For most use cases, we recommend always using the most up-to-date version of R and packages so you have the latest code. In some circumstances (e.g., on a production server or working in a team), you may alternatively want to use specific versions that have been tested to ensure stability. Keeping packages up-to-date is desirable because new code tends to be more efficient, intuitive, robust, and feature-rich. This section explains how.

Previous R versions can be installed from CRAN's archive or previous R releases. The binary versions for all OSes can be found at cran.r-project.org/bin/ (*https://cran.r-project.org/bin/*). To download binary versions for Ubuntu Wily, for example, see *https://cran.r-project.org/bin/linux/ubuntu/wily/*. To pin specific versions of R packages you can use the **packrat** package. For more on pinning R versions and R packages, see the following articles on RStudio's website: Using-Different-Versions-of-R (*http://bit.ly/usingdiffR*) and rstudio.github.io/packrat/ (*https://rstudio.github.io/packrat/*).

Installing R

The method of installing R varies for Windows, Linux, and Mac.

On Windows, a single *.exe* file (hosted at cran.r-project.org/bin/windows/base/ (*https://cran.r-project.org/bin/windows/base/*)) will install the base R package.

On a Mac, the latest version should be installed by downloading the *.pkg* files hosted at *https://cran.r-project.org/bin/macosx/*.

On Linux, the installation method depends on the distribution of Linux installed, though the principles are the same. We'll cover how to install R on Debian-based systems, with links at the end for details on other Linux distributions. The first stage is to add the CRAN (*https://cran.r-project.org/bin/linux/ubuntu/*) repository to ensure that the latest version is installed. If you are running Ubuntu 16.04, for example, append the following line to the file /etc/apt/sources.list:

```
deb http://cran.rstudio.com/bin/linux/ubuntu xenial/
```

http://cran.rstudio.com is the mirror (which can be replaced by any of those listed at *https://cran.r-project.org/mirrors.html*) and xenial is the release. See the Debian (*https://cran.r-project.org/bin/linux/debian/*) and Ubuntu (*https://cran.r-project.org/bin/linux/ubuntu/*) installation pages on CRAN for further details.

Once the appropriate repository has been added and the system updated (e.g., with sudo apt-get update), r-base and other r- packages can be installed using the apt system. The following two commands, for example, would install the base R package (a barebones install) and the package **RCurl**, which has an external dependency:

```
sudo apt-get install r-cran-base # install base R
sudo apt-get install r-cran-rcurl # install the rcurl package
```

apt-cache search "^r-.*" | sort will display all R packages that can be installed from apt in Debian-based systems. In Fedora-based systems, the equivalent command is yum list R-*.

Typical output from the second command is illustrated in the following example:

```
The following extra packages will be installed:
  libcurl3-nss
The following NEW packages will be installed
  libcurl3-nss r-cran-rcurl
0 to upgrade, 2 to newly install, 0 to remove and 16 not to upgrade.
Need to get 699 kB of archives.
After this operation, 2,132 kB of additional disk space will be used.
Do you want to continue? [Y/n]
```

Further details are provided at *https://cran.r-project.org/bin/linux/* for Debian, Redhat, and Suse OSs. R also works on FreeBSD and other Unix-based systems.[3]

Once R is installed, it should be kept up-to-date.

Updating R

R is a mature and stable language, so well-written code in base R should work on most versions. However, it is important to keep your R version relatively up-to-date for the following reasons:

- Bug fixes are introduced in each version, making errors less likely.
- Performance enhancements are made from one version to the next, meaning your code may run faster in later versions.
- Many R packages only work on recent versions on R.

Release notes with details on each of these issues are hosted at *https://cran.r-project.org/src/base/NEWS*. R release versions have three components corresponding to major.minor.patch changes. Generally, two or three patches are released before the next minor increment, each patch is released roughly every three months. R 3.2, for example, has consisted of three versions: 3.2.0, 3.2.1, and 3.2.2.

- On Ubuntu-based systems, new versions of R should be automatically detected through the software management system, and can be installed with `apt-get upgrade`.
- On Mac, the latest version should be installed by the user from the *.pkg* files mentioned previously.
- On Windows, the **installr** package makes updating easy:

  ```
  # check and install the latest R version
  installr::updateR()
  ```

For information about changes to expect in the next version, you can subscribe to R's NEWS RSS feed (*http://bit.ly/RnewsRSS*). It's a good way of keeping up-to-date.

Installing R Packages

Large projects may need several packages to be installed. In this case, the required packages can be installed at once. Using the example of packages for handling spatial data, this can be done quickly and concisely with the following code:

---

3 See Jason French's "Installing R in Linux" (*http://bit.ly/installRlinux*) for more information on installing R on a variety of Linux distributions.

```
pkgs = c("raster", "leaflet", "rgeos") # package names
install.packages(pkgs)
```

In the previous code, all the required packages are installed with two—not three—lines, which reduces typing. Note that we can now reuse the pkgs object to load them all:

```
inst = lapply(pkgs, library, character.only = TRUE) # load them
```

In the previous code, library(pkg[i]) is executed for every package stored in the text string vector. We use library() here instead of require() because the former produces an error if the package is not available.

Loading all packages at the beginning of a script is good practice as it ensures that all dependencies have been installed before time is spent executing code. Storing package names in a character vector object such as pkgs is also useful because it allows us to refer back to them again and again.

Installing R Packages with Dependencies

Some packages have external dependencies (i.e., they call libraries outside R). On Unix-like systems, these are best installed onto the operating system, bypassing install.packages. This will ensure that the necessary dependencies are installed and set up correctly alongside the R package. On Debian-based distributions such as Ubuntu, for example, packages with names starting with r-cran- can be searched for and installed as follows (see *https://cran.r-project.org/bin/linux/ubuntu/* for a list of these):

```
apt-cache search r-cran- # search for available cran Debian packages
sudo apt-get-install r-cran-rgdal # install the rgdal package (with dependencies)
```

On Windows, the **installr** package helps manage and update R packages with system-level dependencies. For example, the **Rtools** package for compiling C/C++ code on Windows can be installed with the following command:

```
installr::install.rtools()
```

Updating R Packages

An efficient R setup will contain up-to-date packages. This can be done for all packages by using:

```
update.packages()
```

The default for this function is for the ask argument to be set to TRUE, giving control over what is downloaded onto your system. This is generally desirable because updating dozens of large packages can consume a large proportion of available system resources.

To update packages automatically, you can add the line `utils::update.packages(ask = FALSE)` to the `.Last` function in the *.Rprofile* startup file (see the next section for more on *.Rprofile*). Thanks to Richard Cotton for this tip.

An even more interactive method for updating packages in R is provided by RStudio via Tools → Check for Package Updates. Many such time-saving tricks are enabled by RStudio, as described in "Installing and Updating RStudio" on page 35. Next (after the exercises), we take a look at how to configure R using startup files.

Exercises

1. What version of R are you using? Is it the most up-to-date?

2. Do any of your packages need updating?

R Startup

Every time R starts, a couple of file scripts are run by default, as documented in `?Startup`. This section explains how to customize these files, allowing you to save API keys or load frequently used functions. Before learning how to modify these files, we'll take a look at how to ignore them, with R's startup arguments. If you want to turn custom setup on, it's useful to be able to turn it off (e.g., for debugging).

 Some of R's startup arguments can be controlled interactively in RStudio. See the online help file Customizing RStudio (*http://bit.ly/ customizeRstudio*) for more on this.

R Startup Arguments

A number of arguments that relate to startup can be appended to the R startup command (`R` in a shell environment). The following are particularly important:

`--no-environ` *and* `--no-init`

Tell R to only look for startup files (described in the next section) in the current working directory.

`--no-restore`

Tells R not to load a file called *.RData* (the default name for R session files) that may be present in the current working directory.

`--no-save`

    Tells R not to ask the user if they want to save objects saved in RAM when the session is ended with q( ).

Adding each of these will make R load slightly faster, meaning that slightly less user input is needed when you quit. R's default setting of loading data from the last session automatically is potentially problematic in this context. See Appendix B of An Introduction to R (*https://cran.r-project.org/doc/manuals/R-intro.pdf*) for more startup arguments.

A concise way to load a vanilla version of R with all of the preceding options enabled is with an option of the same name:

```
R --vanilla
```

An Overview of R's Startup Files

Two files are read each time R starts (unless one of the command-line options outlined previously is used):

.Renviron
    The primary purpose of which is to set *environment variables*. These tell R where to find external programs, and can hold user-specific information that needs to be kept secret, typically *API keys*.

.Rprofile
    A plain text file (which is always called *.Rprofile*, hence its name) that simply runs lines of R code every time R starts. If you want R to check for package updates each time it starts (as explained in the previous section), you simply add the relevant line somewhere in this file.

When R starts (unless it was launched with `--no-environ`), it first searches for *.Renviron* and then *.Rprofile*, in that order. Although *.Renviron* is searched for first, we will look at *.Rprofile* first as it is simpler and, for many setup tasks, more frequently useful. Both files can exist in three directories on your computer.

Modification of R's startup files should not be taken lightly. This is an advanced topic. If you modify your startup files in the wrong way, it can cause problems: a seemingly innocent call to `setwd( )` in *.Rprofile*, for example, will break **devtools** `build` and `check` functions.

Proceed with caution and, if you mess things up, just delete the offending files!

The Location of Startup Files

Confusingly, multiple versions of startup files can exist on the same computer, only one of which will be used per session. Note also that these files should only be changed with caution and if you know what you are doing. This is because they can make your R version behave differently than other R installations, potentially reducing the reproducibility of your code.

Files in three folders are important in this process:

R_HOME

> The directory in which R is installed. The etc subdirectory can contain startup files read early on in the startup process. Find out where your R_HOME is with the R.home() command.

HOME

> The user's home directory. Typically, this is */home/username* on Unix machines or *C:\Users\username* on Windows (since Windows 7). Ask R where your home directory is with Sys.getenv("HOME").

R's current working directory

> This is reported by getwd().

It is important to know the location of the *.Rprofile* and *.Renviron* setup files that are being used out of these three options. R only uses one *.Rprofile* and one *.Renviron* in any session; if you have an *.Rprofile* file in your current project, R will ignore *.Rprofile* in R_HOME and HOME. Likewise, *.Rprofile* in HOME overrides *.Rprofile* in R_HOME. The same applies to *.Renviron*: you should remember that adding project-specific environment variables with *.Renviron* will deactivate other *.Renviron* files.

To create a project-specific startup script, simply create an *.Rprofile* file in the project's root directory and start adding R code (e.g., via file.edit(".Rprofile")). Remember that this will make *.Rprofile* in the home directory be ignored. The following commands will open your *.Rprofile* from within an R editor:

```
file.edit("~/.Rprofile") # edit .Rprofile in HOME
file.edit(".Rprofile") # edit project-specific .Rprofile
```

File paths provided by Windows operating systems will not always work in R. Specifically, if you use a path that contains single backslashes, such as C:\\DATA\\data.csv, as provided by Windows, this will generate the error: Error: unexpected input in "C:\\". To overcome this issue, R provides two functions, file.path() and normalizePath(). The former can be used to specify file locations without having to use symbols to represent relative file paths, as follows: file.path("C:", "DATA", "data.csv"). The latter takes any input string for a filename and outputs a text string that is standard (canonical) for the operating system. normalize Path("C:/DATA/data.csv"), for example, outputs C:\\DATA\ \data.csv on a Windows machine but C:/DATA/data.csv on Unix-based platforms. Note that only the latter would work on both platforms, so standard Unix file path notation is safe for all operating systems.

Editing the *.Renviron* file in the same locations will have the same effect. The following code will create a user-specific *.Renviron* file (where API keys and other cross-project environment variables can be stored) without overwriting any existing file.

```
user_renviron = path.expand(file.path("~", ".Renviron"))
file.edit(user_renviron) # open with another text editor if this fails
```

The **pathological** package can help find where *.Rprofile* and *.Renviron* files are located on your system, thanks to the os_path() function. The output of example(Startup) is also instructive.

The location, contents, and uses of each is outlined in more detail in the next section.

The .Rprofile File

By default, R looks for and runs *.Rprofile* files in the three locations described previously, in a specific order. *.Rprofile* files are simply R scripts that run each time R runs. They can be found within R_HOME, HOME, and the project's home directory by using getwd(). To check if you have a sitewide *.Rprofile*, which will run for all users on startup, run:

```
site_path = R.home(component = "home")
fname = file.path(site_path, "etc", "Rprofile.site")
file.exists(fname)
```

The preceding code code checks for the presence of *Rprofile.site* in that directory. As outlined previously, the *.Rprofile* located in your home directory is user-specific. Again, we can test whether this file exists using:

```
file.exists("~/.Rprofile")
```

We can use R to create and edit .*Rprofile* (warning: do not overwrite your previous .*Rprofile*—we suggest you try project-specific .*Rprofile* first):

```
file.edit("~/.Rprofile")
```

Example .Rprofile File

Example 2-1 provides a taste of what goes into .*Rprofile*. Note that this is simply a usual R script, but with an unusual name. The best way to understand what is going on is to create this same script, save it as .*Rprofile* in your current working directory, and then restart your R session to observe what changes. To restart your R session from within RStudio, you can click Session → Restart R or use the keyboard shortcut Ctrl-Shift-F10.

Example 2-1. Example contents of .Rprofile

```
# A fun welcome message
message("Hi Robin, welcome to R")
# Customize the R prompt that prefixes every command
# (use " " for a blank prompt)
options(prompt = "R4geo> ")
```

Let's quickly explain each line of code. The first simply prints a message in the console each time a new R session is started. The latter modifies the console prompt in the console (set to > by default). Note that simply adding more lines to the .*Rprofile* will set more features. An important aspect of .*Rprofile* (and .*Renviron*) is that *each line is run once and only once for each R session*. That means that the options set within .*Rprofile* can easily be changed during the session. The following command run midsession, for example, will return the default prompt:

```
options(prompt = "> ")
```

More details on these and other potentially useful .*Rprofile* options are described subsequently. For more suggestions of useful startup settings, see examples in help("Startup") and online resources such as those at statmethods.net (*http://www.statmethods.net/interface/customizing.html*). The help pages for R options (accessible with ?options) are also worth a read before writing your own .*Rprofile*.

Ever been frustrated by unwanted + symbols that prevent copied and pasted multiline functions from working? These potentially annoying +s can be eradicated by adding options(continue = " ") to your .*Rprofile*.

Setting options

The function `options` used previously contains a number of default settings. Executing `options()` provides a good indication of what can be configured. The settings that can be configured with `options()` are often related to personal preference (with few implications for reproducibility) so the .*Rprofile* in your home directory is a sensible places to set them if you want them to be set for all your projects that have no project-specific .*Rprofile* file. Other illustrative options are shown here:

```
# With a customized prompt
options(prompt = "R> ", digits = 4, show.signif.stars = FALSE, continue = "  ")
# With a longer prompt and empty 'continue' indent (default is "+ ")
options(prompt = "R4Geo> ", digits = 3, continue = "  ")
```

The first option changes four default options in a single line:

- The R prompt, from the boring > to the exciting R>
- The number of digits displayed
- Removing the stars after significant *p*-values
- Removing the + in multiline functions

Try to avoid adding options that make your code nonportable to the startup file. For example, adding `options(stringsAsFactors = FALSE)` to your startup script has additional effects for `read.table()` and related functions, including `read.csv()`, making them convert text strings into characters rather than into factors, as is the default. This may be useful for you, but it can also make your code less portable, so be warned.

Setting the CRAN mirror

To avoid setting the CRAN mirror each time you run `install.packages()`, you can permanently set the mirror in your .*Rprofile*.

```
# `local` creates a new, empty environment
# This avoids polluting .GlobalEnv with the object r
local({
  r = getOption("repos")
  r["CRAN"] = "https://cran.rstudio.com/"
  options(repos = r)
})
```

The RStudio mirror is a virtual machine run by Amazon's EC2 service, and it syncs with the main CRAN mirror in Austria once per day. Since RStudio is using Amazon's CloudFront, the repository is automatically distributed around the world, so no matter where you are in the world, the data doesn't need to travel very far, and is therefore fast to download.

The fortunes package

This section illustrates the power of *.Rprofile* customization with reference to a package that was developed for fun. The following code could easily be altered to automatically connect to a database, or to ensure that the latest packages have been downloaded.

The **fortunes** package contains a number of memorable quotes, called R fortunes, that the community has collected over many years. Each fortune has a number. To get fortune number 50, for example, enter:

```
fortunes::fortune(50)
#>
#> To paraphrase provocatively, 'machine learning is statistics minus any
#> checking of models and assumptions'.
#>     -- Brian D. Ripley (about the difference between machine learning and
#>        statistics)
#>        useR! 2004, Vienna (May 2004)
```

It is easy to make R print out one of these nuggets of truth each time you start a session by adding the following to *.Rprofile*:

```
if(interactive())
    try(fortunes::fortune(), silent = TRUE)
```

The interactive() function tests whether R is being used interactively in a terminal. The fortune() function is called within try(). If the **fortunes** package is not available, we avoid raising an error and move on. By using ::, we avoid adding the **fortunes** package to our list of attached packages.

 Typing search() gives the list of attached packages. By using for tunes::fortune(), we avoid adding the fortunes package to that list. The function .Last(), if it exists in the *.Rprofile*, is always run at the end of the session. We can use it to install the **fortunes** package if needed. To load the package, we use require(), because if the package isn't installed, the require() function returns FALSE and raises a warning.

```
.Last = function() {
  cond = suppressWarnings(!require(fortunes, quietly = TRUE))
  if(cond)
    try(install.packages("fortunes"), silent = TRUE)
  message("Goodbye at ", date(), "\n")
}
```

Useful functions

You can use *.Rprofile* to define new *helper* functions or redefine existing ones so that they're faster to type. For example, we could load the following two functions for examining data frames:

```
# ht == headtail
ht = function(d, n = 6) rbind(head(d, n), tail(d, n))
# Show the first 5 rows & first 5 columns of a data frame
hh = function(d) d[1:5, 1:5]
```

and a function for setting a nice plotting window:

```
nice_par = function(mar = c(3, 3, 2, 1), mgp = c(2, 0.4, 0), tck = -0.01,
                    cex.axis = 0.9, las = 1, mfrow = c(1, 1), ...) {
    par(mar = mar, mgp = mgp, tck = tck, cex.axis = cex.axis, las = las,
        mfrow = mfrow, ...)
}
```

Note that these functions are for personal use and are unlikely to interfere with code from other people. For this reason, even if you use a certain package every day, we don't recommend loading it in your *.Rprofile*. Shortening long function names for interactive (but not reproducible code writing) is another option for using *.Rprofile* to increase efficiency. If you frequently use View(), for example, you may be able to save time by referring to it in abbreviated form. This is illustrated in the following line of code, which makes it faster to view datasets (although with IDE-driven autocompletion, outlined in the next section, the time savings is less).

```
v = utils::View
```

Also beware of the dangers of loading many functions by default as it may make your code less portable. Another potentially useful setting to change in *.Rprofile* is R's current working directory. If you want R to automatically set the working directory to the R folder of your project, for example, you would add the following line of code to the project-specific *.Rprofile*:

```
setwd("R")
```

Creating hidden environments with .Rprofile

Beyond making your code less portable, another downside of putting functions in your *.Rprofile* is that it can clutter up your workspace: when you run the ls() command, your *.Rprofile* functions will appear. Also, if you run rm(list = ls()), your functions will be deleted. One neat trick to overcome this issue is to use hidden objects and environments. When an object name starts with ., by default it doesn't appear in the output of the ls() function:

```
.obj = 1
".obj" %in% ls()
#> [1] FALSE
```

This concept also works with environments. In the *.Rprofile* file, we can create a *hidden* environment:

```
.env = new.env()
```

And then add functions to this environment:

```
.env$ht = function(d, n = 6) rbind(head(d, n), tail(d, n))
```

At the end of the *.Rprofile* file, we use `attach`, which makes it possible to refer to objects in the environment by their names alone:

```
attach(.env)
```

The .Renviron File

The *.Renviron* file is used to store system variables. It follows a similar startup routine to the *.Rprofile* file: R first looks for a global *.Renviron* file, then for local versions. A typical use of the *.Renviron* file is to specify the R_LIBS path, which determines where new packages are installed:

```
# Linux
R_LIBS=~/R/library
# Windows
R_LIBS=C:/R/library
```

After setting this, `install.packages()` saves packages in the directory specified by R_LIBS. The location of this directory can be referred back to subsequently as follows:

```
Sys.getenv("R_LIBS")
```

All currently stored environment variables can be seen by calling `Sys.getenv()` with no arguments. Note that many environment variables are already preset and do not need to be specified in *.Renviron*. HOME, for example, which can be seen with `Sys.getenv("HOME")`, is taken from the operating system's list of environment variables. A list of the most important environment variables that can affect R's behavior is documented in the little-known help page `help("environment variables")`.

To set or unset an environment variable for the duration of a session, use the following commands:

```
Sys.setenv("TEST" = "test-string") # set an environment variable for the session
Sys.unsetenv("TEST") # unset it
```

Another common use of *.Renviron* is to store API keys and authentication tokens that will be available from one session to another.[4] A common use case is setting the environment variable GITHUB_PAT, which will be detected by the **devtools** package via the

---

4 See `vignette("api-packages")` (*https://cran.r-project.org/web/packages/httr/vignettes/api-packages.html*) from the **httr** package for more on this.

function `github_pat()`. To take another example, the following line in *.Renviron* sets the `ZEIT_KEY` environment variable, which is used in the **diezeit** (*https://cran.r-project.org/web/packages/diezeit/*) package:

```
ZEIT_KEY=PUT_YOUR_KEY_HERE
```

You will need to sign in and start a new R session for the environment variable (accessed by `Sys.getenv()`) to be visible. To test if the example API key has been successfully added as an environment variable, run the following:

```
Sys.getenv("ZEIT_KEY")
```

Using the *.Renviron* file for storing settings such as library paths and API keys is efficient because it reduces the need to update your settings for every R session. Furthermore, the same *.Renviron* file will work across different platforms, so keep it stored safely.

Example .Renviron file

My *.Renviron* file has grown over the years. I often switch between my desktop and laptop computers, so to maintain a consistent working environment, I have the same *.Renviron* file on all of my machines. As well as containing an `R_LIBS` entry and some API keys, my *.Renviron* has a few other lines:

`TMPDIR=/data/R_tmp/`
> When R is running, it creates temporary copies. On my work machine, the default directory is a network drive.

`R_COMPILE_PKGS=3`
> Byte compile all packages (covered in Chapter 3).

`R_LIBS_SITE=/usr/lib/R/site-library:/usr/lib/R/library`
> I explicitly state where to look for packages. My university has a sitewide directory that contains outdated packages. I want to avoiding using this directory.

`R_DEFAULT_PACKAGES=utils,grDevices,graphics,stats,methods`
> Explicitly state the packages to load. Note that I don't load the **datasets** package, but I ensure that **methods** is always loaded. Due to historical reasons, the **methods** package isn't loaded by default in certain applications (e.g., `Rscript`).

Exercises

1. What are the three locations where the startup files are stored? Where are these locations on your computer?

2. For each location, does a *.Rprofile* or *.Renviron* file exist?

3. Create a *.Rprofile* file in your current working directory that prints the message `Happy efficient R programming` each time you start R at this location.

4. What happens to the startup files in `R_HOME` if you create them in `HOME` or local project directories?

RStudio

RStudio is an IDE for R. It makes life easy for R users and developers with its intuitive and flexible interface. RStudio encourages good programming practice. Through its wide range of features, RStudio can help make you a more efficient and productive R programmer. RStudio can, for example, greatly reduce the amount of time spent remembering and typing function names thanks to intelligent autocompletion. Some of the most important features of RStudio include:

- Flexible window pane layouts to optimize use of screen space and enable fast interactive visual feedback

- Intelligent autocompletion of function names, packages, and R objects

- A wide range of keyboard shortcuts

- Visual display of objects, including a searchable data display table

- Real-time code checking, debugging, and error detection

- Menus to install and update packages

- Project management and integration with version control

- Quick display of function source code and help documents

The preceding list of features should make it clear that a well set-up IDE can be as important as a well set-up R installation for becoming an efficient R programmer.[5] As with R itself, the best way to learn about RStudio is by using it. It is therefore worth reading through this section in parallel with using RStudio to boost your productivity.

Installing and Updating RStudio

RStudio is a mature, feature-rich, and powerful IDE optimized for R programming, which has become popular among R developers. The Open Source Edition is completely open source (as can be seen from the project's GitHub rep). It can be installed

---

5 Other open source R IDEs exist, including RKWard (*https://rkward.kde.org/*), Tinn-R (*http://sourceforge.net/projects/tinn-r/*), and JGR (*https://www.rforge.net/JGR/*). emacs (*https://www.gnu.org/software/emacs/*) is another popular software environment. However, it has a very steep learning curve.

on all major OSs from the RStudio website (*https://www.rstudio.com/products/rstudio/download/*).

If you already have RStudio and would like to update it, simply click Help → Check for Updates in the menu. For fast and efficient work, keyboard shortcuts should be used wherever possible, reducing the reliance on the mouse. RStudio has many keyboard shortcuts that will help with this. To get into good habits early, try accessing the RStudio Update interface without touching the mouse. On Linux and Windows, drop-down menus are activated with the Alt key, so the menu item can be found with: Alt-H-U.

On Mac, it works differently. Cmd-? should activate a search across menu items, allowing the same operation to be achieved with Cmd-? update.

 In RStudio, the keyboard shortcuts differ between Linux and Windows versions on one hand and Mac on the other. In this section, we generally only use the Windows/Linux shortcut keys for brevity. The Mac equivalent is usually found by simply replacing Ctrl and Alt with the Mac-specific Cmd button.

Window Pane Layout

RStudio has four main window *panes* (see Figure 2-2), each of which serves a range of purposes:

The Source pane
> For editing, saving, and dispatching R code to the console (top left). Note that this pane does not exist by default when you start RStudio: it appears when you open an R script (e.g., via File → New File → R Script). A common task in this pane is to send code on the current line to the console, via Ctrl/Cmd-Enter.

The Console pane
> Any code entered here is processed by R, line by line. This pane is ideal for interactively testing ideas before saving the final results in the Source pane above.

The Environment pane (top right)
> Contains information about the current objects loaded in the workspace, including their class, dimension (if they are a data frame), and name. This pane also contains tabbed subpanes with a searchable history that was dispatched to the console and (if applicable to the project) Build and Git options.

The Files pane (bottom right)
> Contains a simple file browser, a Plots tab, Help and Package tabs, and a Viewer for visualizing interactive R output such as those produced by the leaflet package and HTML widgets.

Figure 2-2. RStudio panels

Using each of the panels effectively and navigating between them quickly is a skill that will develop over time, and will only improve with practice.

Exercises

You are developing a project to visualize data. Test out the multipanel RStudio workflow by following these steps:

1. Create a new folder for the input data using the Files pane.

2. Type `downl` in the Source pane and hit Enter to make the function `download.file()` autocomplete. Then type `"`, which will autocomplete to `""`, paste the URL of a file to download (e.g., *https://www.census.gov/2010census/csv/pop_change.csv*) and a filename (e.g., *pop_change.csv*).

3. Execute the full command with Ctrl-Enter:

   ```
   download.file("https://www.census.gov/2010census/csv/pop_change.csv",
                 "extdata/pop_change.csv")
   ```

4. Write and execute a command to read the data, such as

   ```
   pop_change = read.csv("extdata/pop_change.csv", skip = 2)
   ```

5. Use the Environment pane to click on the data object `pop_change`. Note that this runs the command `View(pop_change)`, which launches a data viewing tab in the top left panel, for interactively exploring data frames (see Figure 2-3).

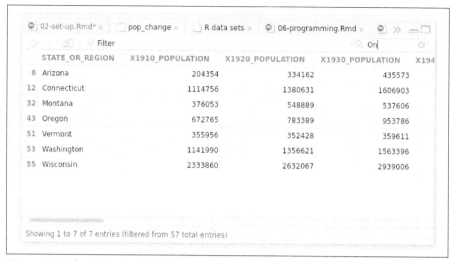

Figure 2-3. The data viewing tab in RStudio

6. Use the console to test different plot commands to visualize the data, saving the code you want to keep back into the Source pane as *pop_change.R*.

7. Use the Plots tab in the Files pane to scroll through past plots. Save the best using the Export drop-down button.

The previous example shows how understanding of these panes and how to use them interactively can help with the speed and productivity of your R programming. Further, there are a number of RStudio settings that can help ensure that it works for your needs.

RStudio Options

A range of project options and global options are available in RStudio from the Tools menu (accessible in Linux and Windows from the keyboard via Alt-T). Most of these are self-explanatory, but it is worth mentioning a few that can boost your programming efficiency:

- GIT/SVN project settings allow RStudio to provide a graphical interface to your version-control system, described in Chapter 9.

- R version settings allow RStudio to point to different R versions/interpreters, which may be faster for some projects.

- `Restore .RData`: untick this default to prevent loading previously created R objects. This will make R start more quickly and also reduce the chance of bugs due to previously created objects. For this reason, we recommend you untick this box.

- Code-editing options can make RStudio adapt to your coding style, for example, by preventing the autocompletion of braces, which some experienced programmers may find annoying. Enabling Vim mode makes RStudio act as a (partial) Vim emulator.

- Diagnostic settings can make RStudio more efficient by adding additional diagnostics or by removing diagnostics if they are slowing down your work. This may be an issue for people using RStudio to analyze large datasets on older low-spec computers.

- Appearance: if you are struggling to see the source code, changing the default font size may make you a more efficient programmer by reducing the time overhead associated with squinting at the screen. Other options in this area relate more to aesthetics. Settings such as font type and background color are also important because feeling comfortable in your programming environment can boost productivity. Go to Tools → Global Options to modify these.

Autocompletion

R provides some basic autocompletion functionality. Typing the beginning of a function name, such as `rn` (short for `rnorm()`), and pressing the Tab key twice will result in the full function names associated with this text string being printed. In this case, two options would be displayed: `rnbinom` and `rnorm`, providing a useful reminder to the user about what is available. The same applies to filenames enclosed in quotation marks: typing `te` in the console in a project that contains a file called *test.R* should result in the full name `"test.R"` being autocompleted. RStudio builds on this functionality and takes it to a new level.

The default settings for autocompletion in RStudio work well. They are intuitive and are likely to work for many users, especially beginners. However, RStudio's autocompletion options can be modified by navigating to Tools → Global Options → Code → Completion in RStudio's top-level menu.

Instead of only autocompleting options when Tab is pressed, RStudio autocompletes them at any point. Building on the previous example, RStudio's autocompletion triggers when the first three characters are typed: `rno`. The same functionality works when only the first characters are typed, followed by Tab: automatic autocompletion does not replace Tab autocompletion but supplements it. Note that in RStudio, two more options are provided to the user after entering `rn` and pressing the Tab key compared with entering the same text into base R's console described in the previous paragraph: `RNGkind` and `RNGversion`. This illustrates that RStudio's autocompletion functionality is not case-sensitive in the same way that R is. This is a good thing because R has no consistent function name style!

RStudio also has more intelligent autocompletion of objects and filenames than R's built-in command line. To test this functionality, try typing US, followed by the Tab key. After pressing down until USArrests is selected, press Enter so it autocompletes. Finally, typing $ should leave the following text on the screen and the four columns should be shown in a dropdown box, ready for you to select the variable of interest with the down arrow.

```
USArrests$ # a drop-down menu of columns should appear in RStudio
```

To take a more complex example, variable names stored in the data slot of the class SpatialPolygonsDataFrame (a class defined by the foundational spatial package **sp**) are referred to in the long form spdf@data$varname.[6] In this case, spdf is the object name, data is the slot, and varname is the variable name. RStudio makes such S4 objects easier to use by enabling autocompletion of the short form spdf$varname. Another example is RStudio's ability to find files hidden away in subfolders. Typing "te will find *test.R* even if it is located in a subfolder such as *R/test.R*. There are a number of other clever autocompletion tricks that can boost R's productivity when using RStudio, which are best found by experimenting and pressing the Tab key frequently during your R programming work.

Keyboard Shortcuts

RStudio has many useful shortcuts that can help make your programming more efficient by reducing the need to reach for the mouse and point and click your way around code and RStudio. These can be viewed by using a little known but extremely useful keyboard shortcut (this can also be accessed via the Tools menu): Alt-Shift-K.

This will display the default shortcuts in RStudio. It is worth spending time identifying which of these could be useful in your work and practicing interacting with RStudio rapidly with minimal reliance on the mouse. The power of these autocompletion capabilities can be further enhanced by setting your own keyboard shortcuts. However, as with setting *.Rprofile* and *.Renviron* settings, this risks reducing the portability of your workflow.

Some more useful (*http://bit.ly/Rstudioshortcuts*) shortcuts are listed here. There are many more gems to find that could boost your R writing productivity:

Ctrl-Z/Shift-Z
    Undo/Redo

---

6 *Slots* are elements of an object (specifically, S4 objects) analogous to a column in a data.frame but referred to with @ not $.

Ctrl-Enter
Execute the current line or code selection in the Source pane

Ctrl-Alt-R
Execute all the R code in the currently open file in the Source pane

Ctrl-Left/Right
Navigate code quickly, word by word

Home/End
Navigate to the beginning/end of the current line

Alt-Shift-Up/Down
Duplicate the current line up or down

Ctrl-D
Delete the current line

To set your own RStudio keyboard shortcuts, navigate to Tools → Modify Keyboard Shortcuts.

Object Display and Output Table

It is useful to know what is in your current R environment. This information can be revealed with `ls()`, but this function only provides object names. RStudio provides an efficient mechanism to show currently loaded objects and their details in real-time: the Environment tab in the top-right corner. It makes sense to keep an eye on which objects are loaded and to delete objects that are no longer useful. Doing so will minimize the probability of confusion in your workflow (e.g., by using the wrong version of an object) and reduce the amount of RAM R needs. The details provided in the Environment tab include the object's dimension and some additional details depending on the object's class (e.g., size in MB for large datasets).

A very useful feature of RStudio is its advanced viewing functionality. This is triggered either by executing `View(object)` or by double-clicking on the object name in the Environment tab. Although you cannot edit data in the Viewer (this should be considered a good thing from a data integrity perspective), recent versions of RStudio provide an efficient search mechanism to rapidly filter and view the records that are of most interest (see Figure 2-3).

Project Management

In the far top-right of RStudio there is a diminutive drop-down menu illustrated with R inside a transparent box. This menu may be small and simple, but it is hugely efficient in terms of organizing large, complex, and long-term projects.

The idea of RStudio projects is that the bulk of R programming work is part of a wider task, which will likely consist of input data, R code, graphical and numerical outputs, and documents describing the work. It is possible to scatter each of these elements at random across your hard disks, but this is not recommended. Instead, the concept of projects encourages reproducible working, such that anyone who opens the particular project folder that you are working from should be able to repeat your analyses and replicate your results.

It is therefore *highly recommended* that you use projects to organize your work. It could save hours in the long run. Organizing data, code, and outputs also makes sense from a portability perspective: if you copy the folder (e.g., via GitHub), you can work on it from any computer without worrying about having the right files on your current machine. These tasks are implemented using RStudio's simple project system, in which the following things happen every time you open an existing project:

- The working directory automatically switches to the project's folder. This enables data and script files to be referred to using relative file paths, which are much shorter than absolute file paths. This means that switching directories using setwd(), a common source of error for R users, is rarely, if ever, needed.
- The last previously open file is loaded into the Source pane. The history of R commands executed in previous sessions is also loaded into the History tab. This assists with continuity between one session and the next.
- The File tab displays the associated files and folders in the project, allowing you to quickly find your previous work.
- Any settings associated with the project, such as Git settings, are loaded. This assists with collaboration and project-specific setup.

Each project is different, but most contain input data, R code, and outputs. To keep things tidy, we recommend a subdirectory structure resembling the following:

```
project/
  - README.Rmd # Project description
  - set-up.R  # Required packages
  - R/ # For R code
  - input # Data files
  - graphics/
  - output/ # Results
```

Proper use of projects ensures that all R source files are neatly stashed in one folder with a meaningful structure. This way, data and documentation can be found where one would expect them. Under this system, figures and project outputs are *first-class citizens* within the project's design, each with their own folder.

Another approach to project management is to treat projects as R packages. This is not recommended for most use cases, as it places restrictions on where you can put files. However, if the aim is code development and sharing, creating a small R package may be the way forward, even if you never intend to submit it on CRAN. Creating R packages is easier than ever before, as documented in *Learning R* by Richard Cotton (O'Reilly) and, more recently, in *R Packages* by Hadley Wickham (O'Reilly). The **devtools** package helps manage R's quirks, making the process much less painful. If you use GitHub, the advantage of this approach is that anyone should be able to reproduce your work using `devtools::install_github("username/projectname")`, although the administrative overhead of creating an entire package for each small project will outweigh the benefits for many.

Note that a *set-up.R* or even a *.Rprofile* file in the project's root directory enables project-specific settings to be loaded each time people work on the project. As described in the previous section, *.Rprofile* can be used to tweak how R works at startup. It is also a portable way to manage R's configuration on a project-by-project basis.

Another capability that RStudio has is excellent debugging support. Rather than reinvent the wheel, I would like to direct interested readers to the RStudio website (*http://bit.ly/debugRstudio*).

Exercises

1. Try modifying the look and appearance of your RStudio setup.

2. What is the keyboard shortcut to show the other shortcut? (Hint: it begins with Alt-Shift on Linux and Windows.)

3. Try as many of the shortcuts revealed by the previous step as you like. Write down the ones that you think will save you time, perhaps on a Post-it note to go on your computer.

BLAS and Alternative R Interpreters

In this section, we cover a few system-level options available to speed up R's performance. Note that for many applications, stability rather than speed is a priority, so these should only be considered if a) you have exhausted options for writing your R code more efficiently and b) you are confident tweaking system-level settings. This should therefore be seen as an advanced section: if you are not interested in speeding up base R, feel free to skip to the next section.

Many statistical algorithms manipulate matrices. R uses the Basic Linear Algebra System (BLAS) framework for linear algebra operations. Whenever we carry out a matrix operation, such as transpose or finding the inverse, we use the underlying BLAS library. By switching to a different BLAS library, it may be possible to speed up your R code. Changing your BLAS library is straightforward if you are using Linux, but can be tricky for Windows users.

The two open source alternative BLAS libraries are ATLAS (*http://math-atlas.sourceforge.net/*) and OpenBLAS (*https://github.com/xianyi/OpenBLAS*). The Intel MKL (*https://software.intel.com/en-us/intel-mkl*) is another implementation, designed for Intel processors by Intel and used in Revolution R (described in the next section), but it requires licensing fees. The MKL library is provided with the Revolution analytics system. Depending on your application, by switching your BLAS library, linear algebra operations can run several times faster than with the base BLAS routines.

If you use Linux, you can find whether you have a BLAS library setting with the following function, from **benchmarkme**:

```
library("benchmarkme")
get_linear_algebra()
```

Testing Performance Gains from BLAS

As an illustrative test of the performance gains offered by BLAS, the following test was run on a new laptop running Ubuntu 15.10 on a sixth-generation Core i7 processor, before and after OpenBLAS was installed.[7]

```
res = benchmark_std() # run a suite of tests to test R's performance
```

It was found that the installation of OpenBLAS led to a two-fold speed-up (from around 150 to 70 seconds). The majority of the speed gain was from the matrix algebra tests, as can be seen in Figure 2-4. Note that the results of such tests are highly dependent on the particularities of each computer. However, it clearly shows that *programming* benchmarks (e.g., the calculation of 3,500,000 Fibonacci numbers) are now much faster, whereas matrix calculations and functions receive a substantial speed boost. This demonstrates that the speed-up you can expect from BLAS depends heavily on the type of computations you are undertaking.

---

7 OpenBLAS was installed on the computer via `sudo apt-get install libopenblas-base`, which is automatically detected and used by R.

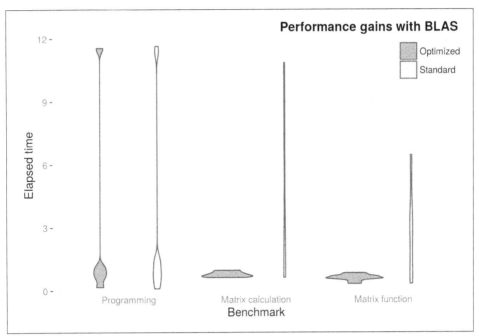

Figure 2-4. Performance gains obtained by changing the underlying BLAS library (tests from benchmark_std())

Other Interpreters

The R language can be separated from the R interpreter. The former refers to the meaning of R commands, and the latter refers to how the computer executes the commands. Alternative interpreters have been developed to try to make R faster and, while promising, none of the following options has fully taken off.

- Microsoft R Open (*http://www.revolutionanalytics.com/microsoft-r-open*), formerly known as Revolution R Open (RRO), is the enhanced distribution of R from Microsoft. The key enhancement is that it uses multithreaded mathematics libraries, which can improve performance.

- Rho (*https://github.com/rho-devel/rho*) (previously called CXXR, short for C++), a reimplementation of the R interpreter for speed and efficiency. Of the new interpreters, this is the one that has the most recent development activity (as of April 2016).

- pqrR (*http://www.pqr-project.org/*) (pretty quick R) is a new version of the R interpreter. One major downside is that it is based on R-2.15.0. The developer (Radford Neal) has made many improvements, some of which have now been incorporated into base R. **pqR** is an open source project licensed under the GPL. One notable improvement in pqR is that it is able to do some numeric computations in parallel with each other, and with other operations of the interpreter, on systems with multiple processors or processor cores.

- Renjin (*http://www.renjin.org/*) reimplements the R interpreter in Java, so it can run on the Java Virtual Machine (JVM). Since R will be pure Java, it can run anywhere.

- Tibco (*http://spotfire.tibco.com/*) created a C++ based interpreter called TERR.

- Oracle also offers an R interpreter that uses Intel's mathematics library and therefore achieves higher performance without changing R's core.

At the time of writing, switching interpreters is something to consider carefully. But in the future, it may become more routine.

Useful BLAS/Benchmarking Resources

- The gcbd (*https://cran.r-project.org/web/packages/gcbd/*) package benchmarks performance of a few standard linear algebra operations across a number of different BLAS libraries as well as a GPU implementation. It has an excellent vignette summarizing the results.

- Brett Klamer (*http://brettklamer.com/diversions/statistical/faster-blas-in-r/*) provides a nice comparison of ATLAS, OpenBLAS, and Intel MKL BLAS libraries. He also gives a description of how to install the different libraries.

- The official R manual section (*https://cran.r-project.org/doc/manuals/r-release/R-admin.html#BLAS*) on BLAS.

Exercise

1. What BLAS system is your version of R using?

References

Cotton, Richard. 2013. *Learning R*. O'Reilly Media.

Wickham, Hadley. 2015c. *R Packages*. O'Reilly Media.

## CHAPTER 3

Efficient Programming

Many people who use R would not describe themselves as programmers. Instead, they tend to have advanced domain-level knowledge and understand standard R data structures such as vectors and data frames, but have little formal training in computing. Sound familiar? In that case, this chapter is for you.

In this chapter, we will discuss "big picture" programming techniques. We cover general concepts and R programming techniques about code optimization, before describing idiomatic programming structures. We conclude the chapter by examining relatively easy ways of speeding up code using the **compiler** package and parallel processing using multiple CPUs.

Prerequisites

In this chapter, we introduce two new packages, **compiler** and **memoise**. The **compiler** package comes with R, so it will already be installed.

```
library("compiler")
library("memoise")
```

We also use the **pryr** and **microbenchmark** packages in the exercises.

Top Five Tips for Efficient Programming

1. Be careful never to grow vectors.

2. Vectorize code whenever possible.

3. Use factors when appropriate.

4. Avoid unnecessary computation by caching variables.

5. Byte compile packages for an easy performance boost.

General Advice

Low-level languages like C and Fortran demand more from the programmer. They force you to declare the type of every variable used, give you the burdensome responsibility of memory management, and have to be compiled. The advantage of such languages, compared with R, is that they are faster to run. The disadvantage is that they take longer to learn and cannot be run interactively.

 The Wikipedia page on compiler optimizations (*https://en.wikipedia.org/wiki/Optimizing_compiler*) gives a nice overview of standard optimization techniques.

R users don't tend to worry about data types. This is advantageous in terms of creating concise code, but can result in R programs that are slow. While optimizations such as going parallel can double speed, poor code can easily run hundreds of times slower, so it's important to understand the causes of slow code. These are covered in *The R Inferno* by Patrick Burns (Lulu.com), which should be considered essential reading for any aspiring R programmer.

Ultimately, calling an R function always ends up calling some underlying C/Fortran code. For example, the base R function `runif()` only contains a single line that consists of a call to `C_runif()`.

```
function (n, min = 0, max = 1)
    .Call(C_runif, n, min, max)
```

A golden rule in R programming is to access the underlying C/Fortran routines as quickly as possible; the fewer function calls required to achieve this, the better. For example, suppose *x* is a standard vector of length *n*. Then

```
x = x + 1
```

involves a single function call to the + function. Whereas the `for` loop

```
for(i in seq_len(n))
    x[i] = x[i] + 1
```

has

- `n` function calls to +

- `n` function calls to the [function

- n function calls to the [<- function (used in the assignment operation)
- A function call to for and to the : operator

It isn't that the for loop is slow; rather it is because we have many more function calls. Each individual function call is quick, but the total combination is slow.

Everything in R is a function call. When we execute 1 + 1, we are actually executing +(1, 1).

Exercise

1. Use the **microbenchmark** package to compare the vectorized construct x = x + 1 to the for loop version. Try varying the size of the input vector.

Memory Allocation

Another general technique is to be careful with memory allocation. If possible, preallocate your vector and then fill in the values.

You should also consider preallocating memory for data frames and lists. Never grow an object. A good rule of thumb is to compare your objects before and after a for loop; have they increased in length?

Let's consider three methods of creating a sequence of numbers. Method 1 creates an empty vector and gradually increases (or grows) the length of the vector:

```
method1 = function(n) {
  vec = NULL # Or vec = c()
  for(i in seq_len(n))
    vec = c(vec, i)
  vec
}
```

Method 2 creates an object of the final length and then changes the values in the object by subscripting:

```
method2 = function(n) {
  vec = numeric(n)
  for(i in seq_len(n))
    vec[i] = i
  vec
}
```

Method 3 directly creates the final object:

```
method3 = function(n) seq_len(n)
```

To compare the three methods, we use the microbenchmark() function from the previous chapter:

```
microbenchmark(times = 100, unit = "s",
               method1(n), method2(n), method3(n))
```

Table 3-1 shows the timing in seconds on my machine for these three methods for a selection of values of n. The relationships for varying n are all roughly linear on a log-log scale, but the timings between methods are drastically different. Notice that the timings are no longer trivial. When $n = 10^7$, method 1 takes around an hour whereas method 2 takes two seconds and method 3 is almost instantaneous. Remember the golden rule: access the underlying C/Fortran code as quickly as possible.

Table 3-1. Time in seconds to create sequences. When n = 10⁷, method 1 takes around an hour while the other methods take less than three seconds.

n	Method 1	Method 2	Method 3
10^5	0.21	0.02	0.00
10^6	25.50	0.22	0.00
10^7	3827.00	2.21	0.00

Vectorized Code

Technically x = 1 creates a vector of length 1. In this section, we use *vectorized* to indicate that functions work with vectors of all lengths.

Recall the golden rule in R programming: access the underlying C/Fortran routines as quickly as possible—the fewer functions calls required to achieve this, the better. With this mind, many R functions are *vectorized*; that is, the function's inputs and/or outputs naturally work with vectors, reducing the number of function calls required. For example, the code

```
x = runif(n) + 1
```

performs two vectorized operations. First, runif() returns n random numbers. Second, we add 1 to each element of the vector. In general, it is a good idea to exploit vectorized functions. Consider this piece of R code that calculates the sum of log (*x*):

```
log_sum = 0
for(i in 1:length(x))
   log_sum = log_sum + log(x[i])
```

Using `1:length(x)` can lead to hard-to-find bugs when x has length zero. Instead, use `seq_along(x)` or `seq_len(length(x))`.

This code could easily be vectorized via

```
log_sum = sum(log(x))
```

Writing code this way has a number of benefits:

- It's faster. When n = 10^7 the *R way* is about 40 times faster.
- It's neater.
- It doesn't contain a bug when x is of length 0.

As with the general example in "General Advice" on page 48, the slowdown isn't due to the for loop. Instead, it's because there are many more functions calls.

Exercises

1. Time the two methods for calculating the log sum.
2. What happens when the `length(x)` = 0 (i.e., we have an empty vector)?

Example: Monte Carlo integration

It's also important to make full use of R functions that use vectors. For example, suppose we wish to estimate the integral $\int_0^1 x^2 \, dx$ using a Monte Carlo method. Essentially, we throw darts at the curve and count the number of darts that fall below the curve (as in Figure 3-1).

Monte Carlo integration

1. Initialize: `hits = 0`
2. for i in 1:N
   a. Generate two random numbers, U_1, U_2, between 0 and 1
   b. If $U_2 < U_1^2$, then `hits = hits + 1`
3. end for
4. Area estimate = `hits/N`

Implementing this Monte Carlo algorithm in R would typically lead to something like:

```
monte_carlo = function(N) {
  hits = 0
  for (i in seq_len(N)) {
    u1 = runif(1)
    u2 = runif(1)
    if (u1 ^ 2 > u2)
      hits = hits + 1
  }
  return(hits / N)
}
```

In R, this takes a few seconds:

```
N = 500000
system.time(monte_carlo(N))
#>    user  system elapsed
#>   2.828   0.008   2.842
```

In contrast, a more R-centric approach would be:

```
monte_carlo_vec = function(N) mean(runif(N)^2 > runif(N))
```

The monte_carlo_vec() function contains (at least) four aspects of vectorization:

- The runif() function call is now fully vectorized.
- We raise entire vectors to a power via ^.
- Comparisons using > are vectorized.
- Using mean() is quicker than an equivalent for loop.

The function monte_carlo_vec() is around 30 times faster than monte_carlo().

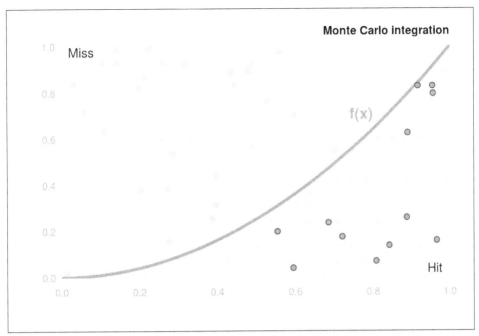

Figure 3-1. Example of Monte Carlo integration. To estimate the area under the curve, throw random points at the graph and count the number of points that lie under the curve.

Exercise

1. Verify that `monte_carlo_vec()` is faster than `monte_carlo()`. How does this relate to the number of darts (i.e., the size of N) that is used?

Communicating with the User

When we create a function, we often want the function to give efficient feedback on the current state. For example, are there missing arguments or has a numerical calculation failed? There are three main techniques for communicating with the user.

Fatal Errors: stop()

Fatal errors are raised by calling `stop()` (i.e., execution is terminated). When `stop()` is called, there is no way for a function to continue. For instance, when we generate random numbers using `rnorm()`, the first argument is the sample size, n. If the number of observations to return is less than 1, an error is raised. When we need to raise an error, we should do so as quickly as possible; otherwise, it's a waste of resources. Hence, the first few lines of a function typically perform argument checking.

Suppose we call a function that raises an error. What then? Efficient, robust code catches the error and handles it appropriately. Errors can be caught using try() and tryCatch(). For example,

```
# Suppress the error message
good = try(1 + 1, silent = TRUE)
bad = try(1 + "1", silent = TRUE)
```

When we inspect the objects, the variable good just contains the number 2:

```
good
#> [1] 2
```

However, the bad object is a character string with class try-error and a condition attribute that contains the error message:

```
bad
#> [1] "Error in 1 + \"1\" : non-numeric argument to binary operator\n"
#> attr(,"class")
#> [1] "try-error"
#> attr(,"condition")
#> <simpleError in 1 + "1": non-numeric argument to binary operator>
```

We can use this information in a standard conditional statement:

```
if(class(bad) == "try-error")
    # Do something
```

Further details on error handling, as well as some excellent advice on general debugging techniques, are given in *Advanced R* by Hadley Wickham (CRC Press).

Warnings: warning()

Warnings are generated using the warning() function. When a warning is raised, it indicates potential problems. For example, mean(NULL) returns NA and also raises a warning.

When we come across a warning in our code, it is important to solve the problem and not just ignore the issue. While ignoring warnings saves time in the short term, warnings can often mask deeper issues that have crept into our code.

 Warnings can be hidden using suppressWarnings().

Informative Output: message() and cat()

To give informative output, use the `message()` function. For example, in the **poweR-law** package, the `message()` function is used to give the user an estimate of expected run time. Providing a rough estimate of how long the function takes allows the user to optimize their time. Similar to warnings, messages can be suppressed with `sup pressMessages()`.

Another function used for printing messages is `cat()`. In general, `cat()` should only be used in `print()`/`show()` methods. For example, look at the function definition of the S3 print method for `difftime` objects: `getS3method("print", "difftime")`.

Exercise

1. The `stop()` function has an argument `call.` that indicates if the function call should be part of the error message. Create a function and experiment with this option.

Invisible Returns

The `invisible()` function allows you to return a temporarily invisible copy of an object. This is particularly useful for functions that return values that can be assigned, but are not printed when they are not assigned. For example, suppose we have a function that plots the data and fits a straight line:

```
regression_plot = function(x, y, ...) {
  # Plot and pass additional arguments to default plot method
  plot(x, y, ...)

  # Fit regression model
  model = lm(y ~ x)

  # Add line of best fit to the plot
  abline(model)
  invisible(model)
}
```

When the function is called, a scattergraph is plotted with the line of best fit, but the output is invisible. However, when we assign the function to an object (i.e., `out = regression_plot(x, y)`), the variable `out` contains the output of the `lm()` call.

Another example is `hist()`. Typically, we don't want anything displayed in the console when we call the function:

```
hist(x)
```

However, if we assign the output to an object, out = hist(x), the object out is actually a list containing, *inter alia*, information on the midpoints, breaks, and counts.

Factors

Factors are much maligned objects. While at times they are awkward, they do have their uses. A factor is used to store categorical variables. This data type is unique to R (or at least not common among programming languages). The difference between factors and strings is important because R treats factors and strings differently. Although factors look similar to character vectors, they are actually integers. This leads to initially surprising behavior:

```
x = 4:6
c(x)
#> [1] 4 5 6
c(factor(x))
#> [1] 1 2 3
```

In this case, the c() function is using the underlying integer representation of the factor. Dealing with the wrong case of behavior is a common source of inefficiency for R users.

Often, categorical variables get stored as 1, 2, 3, 4, and 5, with associated documentation elsewhere that explains what each number means. This is clearly a pain. Alternatively, we store the data as a character vector. While this is fine, the semantics are wrong because it doesn't convey that this is a categorical variable. It's not sensible to say that you should *always* or *never* use factors, since factors have both positive and negative features. Instead, we need to examine each case individually.

As a general rule, if your variable has an inherent order (e.g., small versus large) or you have a fixed set of categories, then you should consider using a factor.

Inherent Order

Factors can be used for ordering in graphics. For instance, suppose we have a dataset where the variable type takes one of three values, small, medium, or large. Clearly, there is an ordering. Using a standard boxplot() call,

```
boxplot(y ~ type)
```

would create a boxplot where the x-axis was alphabetically ordered. By converting type into a factor, we can easily specify the correct ordering.

```
boxplot(y ~ factor(type, levels = c("Small", "Medium", "Large")))
```

Most users interact with factors via the `read.csv()` function, where character columns are automatically converted to factors. This feature can be irritating if our data is messy and we want to clean and recode variables. Typically when reading in data via `read.csv()`, we use the `stringsAsFactors = FALSE` argument. Although this argument can be added to the global `options()` list and placed in the *.Rprofile*, this leads to nonportable code, so should be avoided.

Fixed Set of Categories

Suppose our dataset relates to months of the year:

```
m = c("January", "December", "March")
```

If we sort `m` in the usual way, `sort(m)`, we perform standard alphanumeric ordering; placing `December` first. This is technically correct, but not that helpful. We can use factors to remedy this problem by specifying the admissible levels:

```
# month.name contains the 12 months
fac_m = factor(m, levels = month.name)
sort(fac_m)
#> [1] January  March    December
#> 12 Levels: January February March April May June July August ... December
```

Exercise

1. Factors are slightly more space-efficient than characters. Create a character vector and corresponding factor, and use `pryr::object_size()` to calculate the space needed for each object.

The Apply Family

The apply functions can be an alternative to writing for loops. The general idea is to apply (or map) a function to each element of an object. For example, you can apply a function to each row or column of a matrix. A list of available functions and their descriptions is given in Table 3-2. In general, all apply functions have similar properties:

- Each function takes at least two arguments: an object and another function. The function is passed as an argument.
- Every apply function has the dots (...) argument, which is used to pass on arguments to the function provided to the FUN argument. `sapply(list((1:3)^2, 2:7), mean, trim = 0.4)`, for example, passes the trip argument to the mean function call for each vector in the list.

Using apply functions when possible can lead to shorter, more succinct, idiomatic R code. In this section, we will cover the three main functions, `apply()`, `lapply()`, and `sapply()`. Since the apply functions are covered in most R textbooks, we just give a brief introduction to the topic and provide pointers to other resources at the end of this section.

 Most people rarely use the other apply functions. For example, I have only used `eapply()` once. Students in my class uploaded R scripts. Using `source()`, I was able to read in the scripts to a separate environment. I then applied a marking scheme to each environment using `eapply()`. Using separate environments, I avoided object name clashes.

Table 3-2. The apply family of functions from base R

Function	Description
apply	Apply functions over array margins
by	Apply a function to a data frame split by factors
eapply	Apply a function over values in an environment
lapply	Apply a function over a list or vector
mapply	Apply a function to multiple list or vector arguments
rapply	Recursively apply a function to a list
tapply	Apply a function over a ragged array

The `apply()` function is used to apply a function to each row or column of a matrix. In many data science problems, this is a common task. For example, to calculate the standard deviation of the row:

```
data("ex_mat", package = "efficient")
# MARGIN=1: corresponds to rows
row_sd = apply(ex_mat, 1, sd)
```

The first argument of `apply()` is the object of interest. The second argument is the `MARGIN`. This is a vector giving the subscripts that the function (the third argument) will be applied over. When the object is a matrix, a margin of 1 indicates rows, and 2 indicates columns. So to calculate the column standard deviations, the second argument is changed to 2:

```
col_med = apply(ex_mat, 2, sd)
```

Additional arguments can be passed to the function that is to be applied to the data. For example, to pass the `na.rm` argument to the `sd()` function, we have:

```
row_sd = apply(ex_mat, 1, sd, na.rm = TRUE)
```

The `apply()` function also works on higher dimensional arrays; a one-dimensional array is a vector, a two-dimensional array is a matrix.

The `lapply()` function is similar to `apply()`. The main differences are that the input types are vectors or lists and the return type is a list. Essentially, we apply a function to each element of a list or vector. The functions `sapply()` and `vapply()` are similar to `lapply()`, but the return type is not necessarily a list.

Example: Movies Dataset

The internet movie database (*http://imdb.com/*) is a website that collects movie data supplied by studios and fans. It is one of the largest movie databases on the web and is maintained by Amazon. The **ggplot2movies** package contains about 60,000 movies stored as a data frame:

```
data(movies, package = "ggplot2movies")
```

Movies are rated between 1 and 10 by fans. Columns 7 to 16 of the `movies` dataset gives the percentage of voters for a particular rating.

```
ratings = movies[, 7:16]
```

For example, 4.5% of voters rated the first movie a 1:

```
ratings[1, ]
#>    r1  r2  r3  r4   r5   r6   r7   r8  r9 r10
#> 1 4.5 4.5 4.5 4.5 14.5 24.5 24.5 14.5 4.5 4.5
```

We can use the `apply()` function to investigate voting patterns. The function `nnet::which.is.max()` finds the maximum position in a vector, but breaks ties at random; `which.max()` just returns the first value. Using `apply()`, we can easily determine the most popular rating for each movie and plot the results:

```
popular = apply(ratings, 1, nnet::which.is.max)
plot(table(popular))
```

Figure 3-2 highlights the fact that voting patterns are clearly not uniform between 1 and 10. The most popular vote is the highest rating, 10. Clearly if you went to the trouble of voting for a movie, it was either very good or very bad (there is also a peak at 1). Rating a movie 7 is also a popular choice (search the web for "most popular number" and you will see that 7 dominates the rankings.)

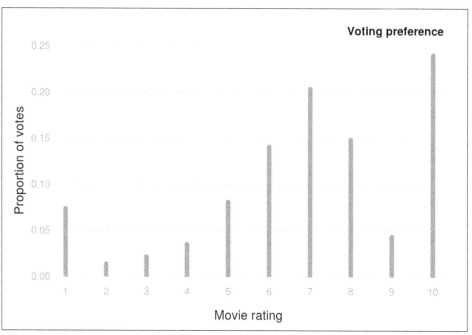

Figure 3-2. Movie voting preferences

Type Consistency

When programming, it is helpful if the return value from a function always takes the same form. Unfortunately, not all base R functions follow this idiom. For example, the functions `sapply()` and `[.data.frame()` aren't type-consistent:

```
two_cols = data.frame(x = 1:5, y = letters[1:5])
zero_cols = data.frame()
sapply(two_cols, class)  # a character vector
sapply(zero_cols, class) # a list
two_cols[, 1:2]          # a data.frame
two_cols[, 1]            # an integer vector
```

This can cause unexpected problems. The functions `lapply()` and `vapply()` are type-consistent, as are `dplyr::select()` and `dplyr:filter()`. The **purrr** package has some type-consistent alternatives to base R functions. For example, you can use `map_dbl()` to replace `Map()`, and `flatten_df()` to replace `unlist()`.

Other resources

Almost every R book has a section on the apply function. Here are resources we feel are most helpful:

- Each function has a number of examples in the associated help page. You can directly access the examples using the `example()` function. For example, to run the `apply()` examples, use `example("apply")`.

- There is a very detailed Stack Overflow answer (*http://bit.ly/sapplyvlapply*) description of when, where, and how to use each of the functions.

- In a similar vein, Neil Saunders has a nice blog post (*http://bit.ly/introapplyR*) giving an overview of the functions.

- The apply functions are an example of functional programming. Chapter 16 of *R for Data Science* by Grolemund and Wickham (O'Reilly) describes the interplay between loops and functional programming in more detail, whereas *Advanced R* by Hadley Wickham (CRC Press) gives a more in-depth description of the topic.

Exercises

1. Rewrite the `sapply()` preceding function calls using `vapply()` to ensure type consistency.

2. How would you make subsetting data frames with [type consistent? Hint: look at the `drop` argument.

Caching Variables

A straightforward method for speeding up code is to calculate objects once and reuse the value when necessary. This could be as simple as replacing `sd(x)` in multiple function calls with the object `sd_x`, which is defined once and reused. For example, suppose we wish to normalize each column of a matrix. However, instead of using the standard deviation of each column, we will use the standard deviation of the entire dataset:

```
apply(x, 2, function(i) mean(i) / sd(x))
```

This is inefficient because the value of `sd(x)` is constant, so recalculating the standard deviation for every column is unnecessary. Instead, we should evaluate once and store the result:

```
sd_x = sd(x)
apply(x, 2, function(i) mean(i) / sd_x)
```

If we compare the two methods on a 100 row by 1,000 column matrix, the cached version is around 100 times faster (Figure 3-3).

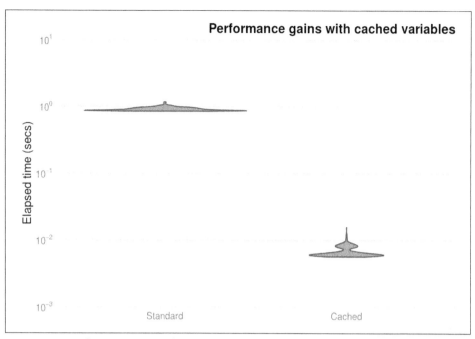

Figure 3-3. Performance gains obtained from caching the standard deviation in a 100 by 1000 matrix

A more advanced form of caching is to use the **memoise** package. If a function is called multiple times with the same input, it may be possible to speed things up by keeping a cache of known answers that it can retrieve. The **memoise** package allows us to easily store the value of a function call and returns the cached result when the function is called again with the same arguments. This package trades off memory versus speed, since the memoised function stores all previous inputs and outputs. To cache a function, we simply pass the function to the **memoise** function.

The classic memoise example is the factorial function. Another example is to limit use to a web resource. For example, suppose we are developing a Shiny (an interactive graphic) application in which the user can fit the regression line to data. The user can remove points and refit the line. An example function would be:

```
# Argument indicates row to remove
plot_mpg = function(row_to_remove) {
  data(mpg, package = "ggplot2")
  mpg = mpg[-row_to_remove, ]
  plot(mpg$cty, mpg$hwy)
  lines(lowess(mpg$cty, mpg$hwy), col = 2)
}
```

We can use **memoise** to speed up by caching results. A quick benchmark

---

```
m_plot_mpg = memoise(plot_mpg)
microbenchmark(times = 10, unit = "ms", m_plot_mpg(10), plot_mpg(10))
#> Unit: milliseconds
#>           expr   min    lq  mean median    uq   max neval cld
#>  m_plot_mpg(10)  0.04 4e-02  0.07  8e-02 8e-02   0.1    10   a
#>    plot_mpg(10) 40.20 1e+02 95.52  1e+02 1e+02 107.1    10   b
```

suggests that we can obtain a 100-fold speed-up.

Exercise

1. Construct a box plot of timings for the standard plotting function and the memoised version.

Function Closures

The following section is meant to provide an introduction to function closures with example use cases. See *Advanced R* by Hadley Wickham (CRC Press) for a detailed introduction.

More advanced caching is available using function closures. A closure in R is an object that contains functions bound to the environment the closure was created in. Technically, all functions in R have this property, but we use the term *function closure* to denote functions where the environment is not in *.GlobalEnv*. One of the environments associated with a function is known as the enclosing environment; that is, where the function was created. This allows us to store values between function calls. Suppose we want to create a stopwatch type function. This is easily achieved with a function closure:

```
# <<- assigns values to the parent environment
stop_watch = function() {
  start_time = NULL
  start = function() start_time <<- Sys.time()
  stop = function() {
    stop_time = Sys.time()
    difftime(stop_time, start_time)
  }
  list(start = start, stop = stop)
}
watch = stop_watch()
```

The object `watch` is a list that contains two functions. One function for starting the timer:

```
watch$start()
```

and the other for stopping the timer:

```
watch$stop()
```

Without using function closures, the stopwatch function would be longer, more complex, and therefore more inefficient. When used properly, function closures are very useful programming tools for writing concise code.

Exercises

1. Write a stopwatch function *without* using function closures.

2. Many stopwatches have the ability to measure not only your overall time but also your individual laps. Add a `lap()` function to the `stop_watch()` function that will record individual times, while still keeping track of the overall time.

 A related idea to function closures is nonstandard evaluation (NSE), or programming on the language. NSE crops up all the time in R. For example, when we execute `plot(height, weight)`, R automatically labels the x- and y-axis of the plot with `height` and `weight`. This is a powerful concept that enables us to simplify code. More detail is given in the "Nonstandard evaluation" section of *Advanced R* by Hadley Wickham.

The Byte Compiler

The **compiler** package, written by R Core member Luke Tierney, has been part of R since version 2.13.0. The **compiler** package allows R functions to be compiled, resulting in a byte code version that may run faster.[1] The compilation process eliminates a number of costly operations the interpreter has to perform, such as variable lookup.

Since R 2.14.0, all of the standard functions and packages in base R are precompiled into byte code. This is illustrated by the base function `mean()`:

```
getFunction("mean")
#> function (x, ...)
#> UseMethod("mean")
#> <bytecode: 0x48eec88>
#> <environment: namespace:base>
```

The third line contains the `bytecode` of the function. This means that the **compiler** package has translated the R function into another language that can be interpreted

---

1 The authors have yet to find a situation where byte-compiled code runs significantly slower.

by a very fast interpreter. Amazingly, the **compiler** package is almost entirely pure R, with just a few C support routines.

Example: The Mean Function

The **compiler** package comes with R, so we just need to load the package in the usual way:

```
library("compiler")
```

Next, we create an inefficient function for calculating the mean. This function takes in a vector, calculates the length, and then updates the m variable.

```
mean_r = function(x) {
  m = 0
  n = length(x)
  for(i in seq_len(n))
    m = m + x[i] / n
  m
}
```

This is clearly a bad function and we should just use the mean() function, but it's a useful comparison. Compiling the function is straightforward:

```
cmp_mean_r = cmpfun(mean_r)
```

Then we use the microbenchmark() function to compare the three variants:

```
# Generate some data
x = rnorm(1000)
microbenchmark(times = 10, unit = "ms", # milliseconds
          mean_r(x), cmp_mean_r(x), mean(x))
#> Unit: milliseconds
#>          expr   min    lq  mean median    uq  max neval cld
#>     mean_r(x) 0.358 0.361 0.370  0.363 0.367 0.43    10   c
#> cmp_mean_r(x) 0.050 0.051 0.052  0.051 0.051 0.07    10   b
#>       mean(x) 0.005 0.005 0.008  0.007 0.008 0.03    10   a
```

The compiled function is around seven times faster than the uncompiled function. Of course, the native mean() function is faster, but compiling does make a significant difference (Figure 3-4).

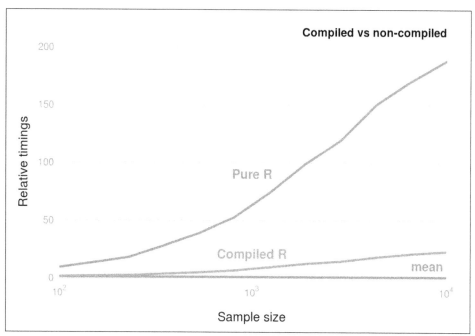

Figure 3-4. Comparsion of mean functions

Compiling Code

There are a number of ways to compile code. The easiest is to compile individual functions using cmpfun(), but this obviously doesn't scale. If you create a package, you can automatically compile the package on installation by adding

```
ByteCompile: true
```

to the DESCRIPTION file. Most R packages installed using install.packages() are not compiled. We can enable (or force) packages to be compiled by starting R with the environment variable R_COMPILE_PKGS set to a positive integer value and specify that we install the package from source:

```
## Windows users will need Rtools
install.packages("ggplot2", type = "source")
```

Or, if we want to avoid altering the *.Renviron* file, we can specify an additional argument:

```
install.packages("ggplot2", type = "source", INSTALL_opts = "--byte-compile")
```

A final option is to use just-in-time (JIT) compilation.[2] The `enableJIT()` function disables JIT compilation if the argument is 0. Arguments 1, 2, or 3 implement different levels of optimization. JIT can also be enabled by setting the environment variable R_ENABLE_JIT to one of these values.

We recommend setting the compile level to the maximum value of 3.

The impact of compiling on install will vary from package to package. For packages that already have lots of precompiled code, speed gains will be small (R Core Team 2016).

Not all packages work when compiled on installation.

References

Burns, Patrick. 2011. *The R Inferno*. Lulu.com.

Wickham, Hadley. 2014a. *Advanced R*. CRC Press.

Grolemund, G., and H. Wickham. 2016. *R for Data Science*. O'Reilly Media.

R Core Team. 2016. "R Installation and Administration." *R Foundation for Statistical Computing. https://cran.r-project.org/doc/manuals/r-release/R-admin.html*.

---

2 It appears that in R 3.4, this optimization will be enabled by default.

## CHAPTER 4

Efficient Workflow

Efficient programming is an important skill for generating the correct result, on time. Yet coding is only one part of a wider skillset needed for successful outcomes for projects involving R programming. Unless your project is to write generic R code (i.e., unless you are on the R Core Team), the project will probably transcend the confines of the R world; it must engage with a whole range of other factors. In this context, we define *workflow* as the sum of practices, habits, and systems that enable productivity.[1] To some extent, workflow is about personal preferences. Everyone's mind works differently so the most appropriate workflow varies from person to person and from one project to the next. Project management practices will also vary depending on the scale and type of the project. It's a big topic, but it can usefully be condensed into five top tips.

Prerequisites

This chapter focuses on workflow. For project planning and management, we'll use the **DiagrammeR** package. For project reporting, we'll focus on R Markdown and **knitr**, which are bundled with RStudio (but can be installed independently if needed). We'll suggest other packages that are worth investigating, but are not required for this particular chapter.

```
library("DiagrammeR")
```

---

1 The Oxford Dictionary's definition of workflow is similar, with a more industrial feel: "The sequence of industrial, administrative, or other processes through which a piece of work passes from initiation to completion."

Top Five Tips for Efficient Workflow

1. Start without writing code but with a clear mind and perhaps a pen and paper. This will ensure that you keep your objectives at the forefront of your mind without getting lost in the technology.

2. Make a plan. The size and nature will depend on the project but timelines, resources, and *chunking* the work will make you more effective when you start.

3. Select the packages you will use for implementing the plan early. Minutes spent researching and selecting from the available options could save hours in the future.

4. Document your work at every stage: work can only be effective if it's communicated clearly and code can only be efficiently understood if it's commented.

5. Make your entire workflow as reproducible as possible. **knitr** can help with this in the phase of documentation.

A Project Planning Typology

Appropriate project management structures and workflow depend on the *type* of project you are undertaking. The following typology demonstrates the links between project type and project management requirements.[2]

Data analysis

Here, you are trying to explore datasets to discover something interesting/answer some questions. The emphasis is on speed of manipulating your data to generate interesting results. Formality is less important in this type of project. Sometimes this analysis project may only be part of a larger project (the data may have to be created in a lab, for example). How the data analysts interact with the rest of the team may be as important for the project's success as how they interact with each other.

Package creation

Here you want to create code that can be reused across projects, possibly by people whose use cases you don't know (if you make it publicly available). The emphasis in this case will be on clarity of user interface and documentation, meaning style and code review are important. Robustness and testing are important in this type of project, too.

---

2 Thanks to Richard Cotton for suggesting this typology.

Reporting and publishing

Here you are writing a report, journal paper, or book. The level of formality varies depending upon the audience, but you have additional worries like how much code it takes to arrive at the conclusions, and how much output the code creates.

Software applications

This could range from a simple Shiny app to R being embedded in the server of a much larger piece of software. Either way, since there is limited opportunity for human interaction, the emphasis is on robust code and gracefully dealing with failure.

Based on these observations, we recommend thinking about which type of workflow, file structure, and project management system suits your project best. Sometimes it's best not to be prescriptive, so we recommend trying different working practices to discover which works best, time permitting.[3]

There are, however, concrete steps that can be taken to improve workflow in most projects that involve R programming. Learning them will, in the long run, improve productivity and reproducibility. With these motivations in mind, the purpose of this chapter is simple: to highlight some key ingredients of an efficient R workflow. It builds on the concept of an R/RStudio *project*, introduced in Chapter 2, and is ordered chronologically throughout the stages involved in a typical project's lifespan, from inception to publication:

Project planning

This should happen before any code has been written, to avoid time wasted using a mistaken analysis strategy. Project management is the art of making project plans happen.

Package selection

After planning your project, you should identify which packages are most suitable to getting the work done quickly and effectively. With rapid increases in the number and performance of packages, it is more important than ever to consider the range of options at the outset. For example, `*_join()` from **dplyr** is often more appropriate than `merge()`, as we'll see in Chapter 6.

Publication

This final stage is relevant if you want your R code to be useful for others in the long term. To this end, "Publication" on page 80 touches on documentation using

---

3 The importance of workflow has not gone unnoticed by the R community, and there are a number of different suggestions to boost R productivity. Rob Hyndman (*http://robjhyndman.com/hyndsight/workflow-in-r/*), for example, advocates the strategy of using four self-contained scripts to break up R work into manageable chunks: `load.R`, `clean.R`, `func.R`, and `do.R`.

knitr and the much stricter approach to code publication of package development.

Project Planning and Management

Good programmers working on a complex project will rarely just start typing code. Instead, they will plan the steps needed to complete the task as efficiently as possible: "smart preparation minimizes work" (Berkun 2005). Although search engines are useful for identifying the appropriate strategy, trial-and-error approaches (e.g., typing code at random and Googling the inevitable error messages) are usually highly *inefficient*.

Strategic thinking is especially important during a project's inception: if you make a bad decision early on, it will have cascading negative impacts throughout the project's entire lifespan. So detrimental and ubiquitous is this phenomenon in software development that a term has been coined to describe it: *technical debt*. This has been defined as "not quite right code which we postpone making right" (Kruchten, Nord, and Ozkaya 2012). Dozens of academic papers have been written on the subject, but from the perspective of *beginning* a project (i.e., in the planning stage, where we are now), all you need to know is that it is absolutely vital to make sensible decisions at the outset. If you do not, your project may be doomed to failure of incessant rounds of refactoring.

To minimize technical debt at the outset, the best place to start may be with a pen and paper and an open mind. Sketching out your ideas and deciding precisely what you want to do, free from the constraints of a particular piece of technology, can be a rewarding exercise before you begin. Project planning and *visioning* can be a creative process not always well-suited to the linear logic of computing, despite recent advances in project management software, some of which are outlined in the bullet points that follow.

Scale can loosely be defined as the number of people working on a project. It should be considered at the outset because the importance of project management increases exponentially with the number of people involved. Project management may be trivial for a small project, but if you expect it to grow, implementing a structured workflow early on could avoid problems later. On small projects consisting of a *one-off* script, project management may be a distracting waste of time. Large projects involving dozens of people, on the other hand, require much effort dedicated to project management: regular meetings, division of labor, and a scalable project management system to track progress, issues, and priorities will inevitably consume a large proportion of the project's time. Fortunately, a multitude of dedicated project management systems have been developed to cater to projects across a range of scales. These include, in rough ascending order of scale and complexity, the following:

- The interactive code-sharing site GitHub (*https://github.com/*), which is described in more detail in Chapter 9

- ZenHub (*https://www.zenhub.io/*), a browser plugin that is "the first and only project management suite that works natively within GitHub"

- Web-based and easy-to-use tools such as Trello (*https://trello.com/*)

- Dedicated desktop project management software such as ProjectLibre (*http://bit.ly/Projectlibre*) and GanttProject (*http://bit.ly/ganttProject*)

- Fully featured, enterprise scale, open source project management systems such as OpenProject (*http://bit.ly/openpro*) and redmine (*http://www.redmine.org/*)

Regardless of the software (or lack thereof) used for project management, it involves considering the project's aims in the context of available resources (e.g., computational and programmer resources), project scope, time scales, and suitable software. And these things should be considered together. To take one example, is it worth the investment of time needed to learn a particular R package that is not essential to completing the project but which will make the code run faster? Does it make more sense to hire another programmer or invest in more computational resources to complete an urgent deadline?

Minutes spent thinking through such issues before writing a single line can save hours in the future. This is emphasized in books such as *The Art of Project Management* by Scott Berkun (O'Reilly) and the "Guide to the Project Management Body of Knowledge" by PMBoK and useful online resources such those by teamgantt.com (*http://teamgantt.com/guide-to-project-management/*) and lasa.org.uk (*http://bit.ly/lasaprojman*), which focus exclusively on project planning. This section condenses some of the most important lessons from this literature in the context of typical R projects (i.e., those that involve data analysis, modeling, and visualization).

Chunking Your Work

Once a project overview has been devised and stored, in mind (for small projects, if you trust that as storage medium!) or written, a plan with a timeline can be drawn up. The up-to-date visualization of this plan can be a powerful reminder to you and collaborators of the progress on the project so far. More importantly, the timeline provides an overview of what needs to be done next. Setting start dates and deadlines for each task will help prioritize the work and ensure that you are on track. Breaking a large project into smaller chunks is highly recommended, making huge, complex tasks more achievable and modular (PMBoK 2000). *Chunking* the work will also make collaboration easier, as we shall see in Chapter 5.

The tasks that a project should be split into will depend on the nature of the work. The phases illustrated in Figure 4-1 represent a rough starting point, not a template.

The *programming* phase will usually need to be split into at least *data tidying*, *processing*, and *visualization*.

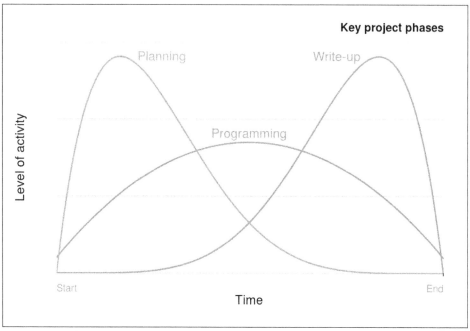

Figure 4-1. Schematic illustrations of key project phases and levels of activity over time, based on the "Guide to the Project Management Body of Knowledge" (PMBoK 2000)

Making Your Workflow SMART

A more rigorous (but potentially onerous) way to project plan is to divide the work into a series of objectives and track their progress throughout the project's duration. One way to check if an objective is appropriate for action and review is by using the SMART criteria:

- Specific: is the objective clearly defined and self-contained?
- Measurable: is there a clear indication of its completion?
- Attainable: can the target be achieved?
- Realistic: have sufficient resources been allocated to the task?
- Time-bound: is there an associated completion date or milestone?

If the answer to each of these questions is yes, the task is likely to be suitable to include in the project's plan. Note that this does not mean all project plans need to be uniform. A project plan can take many forms, including a short document, a Gantt chart (see Figure 4-2), or simply a clear vision of the project's steps in mind.

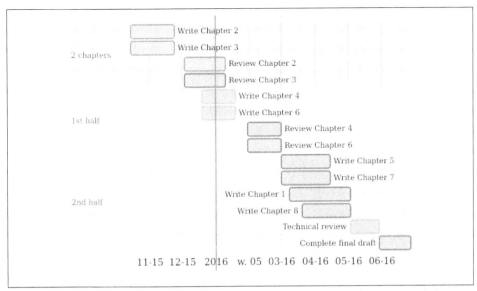

Figure 4-2. A Gantt chart created using DiagrammeR illustrating the steps needed to complete this book at an early stage of its development

Visualizing Plans with R

Various R packages can help visualize the project plan. Though these are useful, they cannot compete with the dedicated project management software outlined at the outset of this section. However, if you are working on a relatively simple project, it is useful to know that R can help represent and keep track of your work. Packages for plotting project progress include:[4]

plan *(https://cran.r-project.org/web/packages/plan/)*
> Provides basic tools to create burndown charts (which concisely show whether a project is on time or not) and Gantt charts.

plotrix *(https://cran.r-project.org/web/packages/plotrix/index.html)*
> A general-purpose plotting package, provides basic Gantt chart-plotting functionality. Enter `example(gantt.chart)` for details.

DiagrammeR *(http://rich-iannone.github.io/DiagrammeR/)*
> A new package for creating network graphs and other schematic diagrams in R. This package provides an R interface to simple flowchart file formats such as

---

4 For a more comprehensive discussion of Gantt charts in R, please refer to *stackoverflow.com/questions/ 3550341* (*http://bit.ly/ganttchartsR*).

mermaid (*https://github.com/knsv/mermaid*) and GraphViz (*https://github.com/ellson/graphviz*).

The small example that follows (which provides the basis for creating charts like Figure 4-2) illustrates how **DiagrammeR** can take simple text inputs to create informative up-to-date Gantt charts. Such charts can greatly help with the planning and task management of long and complex R projects, as long as they do not take away valuable programming time from core project objectives.

```
library("DiagrammeR")
# Define the Gantt chart and plot the result (not shown)
mermaid("gantt
        Section Initiation
        Planning          :a1, 2016-01-01, 10d
        Data processing   :after a1 , 30d")
```

In this example, gantt defines the subsequent data layout. Section refers to the project's section (useful for large projects, with milestones), and each new line refers to a discrete task. Planning, for example, has the code a, begins on the first day of 2016, and lasts for 10 days. See *knsv.github.io/mermaid/gantt.html* for more detailed documentation.

Exercises

1. What are the three most important work *chunks* of your current R project?

2. What is the meaning of *SMART* objectives (see Making Your Workflow SMART)?

3. Run the code chunk at the end of this section to see the output.

4. Bonus exercise: modify this code to create a basic Gantt chart of an R project you are working on.

Package Selection

A good example of the importance of prior planning to minimize effort and reduce technical debt is package selection. An inefficient, poorly supported, or simply outdated package can waste hours. When a more appropriate alternative is available, this waste can be prevented by prior planning. There are many poor packages on CRAN and much duplication so it's easy to go wrong. Just because a certain package *can* solve a particular problem doesn't mean that it *should*.

Used well, however, packages can greatly improve productivity: not reinventing the wheel is part of the ethos of open source software. If someone has already solved a particular technical problem, you don't have to rewrite their code, which allows you to focus on solving the applied problem. Furthermore, because R packages are generally (but not always) written by competent programmers and subject to user feedback, they may work faster and more effectively than the hastily prepared code you may have written. All R code is open source and potentially subject to peer review. A prerequisite of publishing an R package is that developer contact details must be provided, and many packages provide a site for issue tracking. Furthermore, R packages can increase programmer productivity by dramatically reducing the amount of code they need to write because all the code is *packaged* in functions behind the scenes.

Let's look at an example. Imagine a project for which you would like to find the distance between sets of points (origins, o, and destinations, d) on the Earth's surface. Background reading shows that a good approximation of *great circle* distance, which accounts for the curvature of the Earth, can be made by using the Haversine formula, which you duly implement, involving much trial and error:

```
# Function to convert degrees to radians
deg2rad = function(deg) deg * pi / 180

# Create origins and destinations
o = c(lon = -1.55, lat = 53.80)
d = c(lon = -1.61, lat = 54.98)

# Convert to radians
o_rad = deg2rad(o)
d_rad = deg2rad(d)

# Find difference in degrees
delta_lon = (o_rad[1] - d_rad[1])
delta_lat = (o_rad[2] - d_rad[2])

# Calculate distance with Haversine formula
a = sin(delta_lat / 2)^2 + cos(o_rad[2]) * cos(d_rad[2]) * sin(delta_lon / 2)^2
c = 2 * asin(min(1, sqrt(a)))
(d_hav1 = 6371 * c) # multiply by Earth's diameter
#> [1] 131
```

This method works but it takes time to write, test, and debug. It would be much better to package it up into a function. Or even better, use a function that someone else has written and put in a package:

```
# Find great circle distance with geosphere
(d_hav2 = geosphere::distHaversine(o, d))
#> [1] 131415
```

The difference between the hardcoded method and the package method is striking. One is seven lines of tricky R code involving many subsetting stages and small, similar functions (e.g., sin and asin), which are easy to confuse. The other is one line of simple code. The package method using **geosphere** took perhaps 100th of the time *and* gave a more accurate result (because it uses a more accurate estimate of the diameter of the Earth). This means that a couple of minutes searching for a package to estimate great circle distances would have been time well spent at the outset of this project. But how do you search for packages?

Searching for R Packages

Building on the preceding example, how can you find out if there is a package to solve your particular problem? The first stage is to guess: if it is a common problem, someone has probably tried to solve it. The second stage is to search. A simple Google query, `haversine formula R`, returned a link to the **geosphere** package in the second result (a hardcoded implementation (*http://www.r-bloggers.com/great-circle-distance-calculations-in-r/*) was first).

Beyond Google, there are also several sites for searching for packages and functions. rdocumentation.org provides a multifield search environment to pinpoint the function or package you need. Amazingly, the search for `haversine` in the Description field yielded 10 results from eight packages: R has at least eight implementations of the Haversine formula! This shows the importance of careful package selection as there are often many packages that do the same job, as we will see in the next section. There is also a way to find the function from within R, with `RSiteSearch()`, which opens a URL in your browser linking to a number of functions (40) and vignettes (2) that mention the text string:

```
# Search CRAN for mentions of haversine
RSiteSearch("haversine")
```

How to Select a Package

Due to the conservative nature of base R development, which rightly prioritizes stability over innovation, much of the innovation and performance gains in the *R ecosystem* have occurred in recent years in the packages. The increased ease of package development (Wickham 2015c) and interfacing with other languages (Eddelbuettel et al. 2011) has accelerated their number, quality, and efficiency. An additional factor has been the growth in collaboration and peer review in package development, driven by code-sharing websites such as GitHub and online communities such as ROpenSci (*https://ropensci.org/*) for peer reviewing code.

Performance, stability, and ease of use should be high on the priority list when choosing which package to use. Another more subtle factor is that some packages work better together than others. The *R package ecosystem* is composed of interrelated packages. Knowing something of these interdependencies can help you select a *package suite* when the project demands a number of diverse yet interrelated programming tasks. The *tidyverse*, for example, contains many interrelated packages that work well together, such as **readr**, **tidyr**, and **dplyr**.[5] These may be used together to read, tidy, and then process the data, as outlined in the subsequent sections.

There is no hard and fast rule about which package you should use and new packages are emerging all the time. The ultimate test will be empirical evidence: does it get the job done on your data? However, the following criteria should provide a good indication of whether a package is worth an investment of your precious time, or even installing on your computer:

Is it mature?

    The more time a package is available, the more time it will have for obvious bugs to be ironed out. The age of a package on CRAN can be seen from its Archive page on CRAN. We can see from the ggplot2 archive (*http://bit.ly/ggplot2archive*), for example, that **ggplot2** was first released on the June 10, 2007 and that it has had 29 releases. The most recent of these at the time of writing was **ggplot2** 2.1.0; reaching 1 or 2 in the first digit of package versions is usually an indication from the package author that the package has reached a high level of stability.

Is it actively developed?

    It is a good sign if packages are frequently updated. A frequently updated package will have its latest version published recently on CRAN. The CRAN package page for **ggplot2**, for example, said `Published: 2016-03-01`, which was less than six months old at the time of writing.

Is it well documented?

    This is not only an indication of how much thought, care, and attention has gone into the package, it also has a direct impact on its ease of use. Using a poorly documented package can be inefficient due to the hours spent trying to work out how to use it! To check if the package is well documented, look at the help pages associated with its key functions (e.g., `?ggplot`), try the examples (e.g., `example(ggplot)`), and search for package vignettes (e.g., `vignette(package = "ggplot2")`).

Is it well used?

    This can be seen by searching for the package name online. Most packages that have a strong user base will produce thousands of results when typed into a generic search engine such as Google. More specific (and potentially useful) indications of use will narrow down the search to particular users. A package widely used by the programming community will likely be visible on GitHub. At the time of writing, a search for **ggplot2** (*http://bit.ly/ggplot2GH*) on GitHub yielded over 400 repositories and almost 200,000 matches in committed code! Likewise, a

---

5 An excellent overview of the tidyverse, formerly known as the hadleyverse, and its benefits is available from barryrowlingson.github.io/hadleyverse (*https://barryrowlingson.github.io/hadleyverse*).

package that has been adopted for use in academia will tend to be mentioned in Google Scholar (again, **ggplot2** scores extremely well in this measure, with over 5,000 hits).

An article in simplystats (*http://bit.ly/trustRpackage*) discusses this issue with reference to the proliferation of GitHub packages (those that are not available on CRAN). In this context, well-regarded and experienced package creators and indirect data such as the amount of GitHub activity are also highlighted as reasons to trust a package.

The websites of MRAN (*https://mran.revolutionanalytics.com/packages*) and META-CRAN (*http://www.r-pkg.org*) can help the package-selection process by providing further information on each package uploaded to CRAN. METACRAN (*http://www.r-pkg.org*), for example, provides metadata about R packages via a simple API and the provision of badges to show how many downloads a particular package has per month. Returning to the Haversine example given previously, we could find out how many times two packages that implement the formula are downloaded each month with the following URLs:

- `http://cranlogs.r-pkg.org/badges/last-month/geosphere`, downloads of **geosphere**:

downloads 17K/month

- `http://cranlogs.r-pkg.org/badges/last-month/geoPlot`, downloads of **geoPlot**:

downloads 3/month

It is clear from the results reported that **geosphere** is by far the more popular package, so is a sensible and mature choice for dealing with distances on the Earth's surface.

Publication

The final stage in a typical project workflow is publication. Although it's the final stage to be worked on, that does not mean you should only document *after* the other stages are complete: making documentation integral to your overall workflow will make this stage much easier and more efficient.

Whether the final output is a report containing graphics produced by R, an online platform for exploring results, or well-documented code that colleagues can use to improve their workflow, starting it early is a good plan. In every case, the programming principles of reproducibility, modularity, and DRY (don't repeat yourself) will make your publications faster to write, easier to maintain, and more useful to others.

Instead of attempting a comprehensive treatment of the topic, we will touch briefly on a couple of ways of documenting your work in R: dynamic reports and R packages. There is a wealth of material on each of these online. A wealth of online resources exists on each of these; to avoid duplication of effort, the focus is on documentation from a workflow-efficiency perspective.

Dynamic Documents with R Markdown

When writing a report using R outputs, a typical workflow has historically been to 1) do the analysis, 2) save the resulting graphics and record the main results outside the R project, and 3) open a program unrelated to R such as LibreOffice to import and communicate the results in prose. This is inefficient: it makes updating and maintaining the outputs difficult (when the data changes, steps 1 to 3 will have to be done again) and there is overhead involved in jumping between incompatible computing environments.

To overcome this inefficiency in the documentation of R outputs, the R Markdown framework was developed. Used in conjunction with the **knitr** package, we have:

- The ability to process code chunks (via **knitr**)
- A notebook interface for R (via RStudio)
- The ability to render output to multiple formats (via pandoc)

R Markdown documents are plain text and have the file extension *.Rmd*. This framework allows for documents to be generated automatically. Furthermore, *nothing* is efficient unless you can quickly redo it. Documenting your code inside dynamic documents in this way ensures that analysis can be quickly rerun.

 This note briefly explains R Markdown for the uninitiated. R markdown is a form of Markdown. Markdown is a pure text document format that has become a standard for documentation for software. It is the default format for displaying text on GitHub. R Markdown allows the user to embed R code in a Markdown document. This is a powerful addition to Markdown, as it allows custom images, tables, and even interactive visualizations to be included in your R documents. R Markdown is an efficient file format to write in because it is lightweight, human, and computer-readable, and is much less verbose than HTML and LaTeX. The first draft of this book was written in R Markdown.

In an R Markdown document, results are generated on the fly by including *code chunks*. Code chunks are R code that are preceded by ```` ```{r, options} ```` on the line before the R code, and ```` ``` ```` at the end of the chunk. For example, suppose we have the code chunk

```
```{r eval = TRUE, echo = TRUE}
(1:5)^2
```
```

in an R Markdown document. The `eval = TRUE` in the code indicates that the code should be evaluated, while `echo = TRUE` controls whether the R code is displayed. When we compile the document, we get

```
(1:5)^2
#> [1]  1  4  9 16 25
```

R Markdown via **knitr** provides a wide range of options to customize what is displayed and evaluated. When you adapt to this workflow, it is highly efficient, especially as RStudio provides a number of shortcuts that make it easy to create and modify code chunks. To create a chunk while editing an *.Rmd* file, for example, simply enter Ctrl/Cmd-Alt-I on Windows or Linux or select the option from the Code drop-down menu.

Once your document has compiled, it should appear on your screen into the file format requested. If an HTML file has been generated (as is the default), RStudio provides a feature that allows you to put it up online rapidly. This is done using the rpubs (*https://rpubs.com*) website, a store of a huge number of dynamic documents (which could be a good source of inspiration for your publications). Assuming you have an RStudio account, clicking the Publish button at the top of the HTML output window will instantly publish your work online, with a minimum of effort, enabling fast and efficient communication with many collaborators and the public.

An important advantage of dynamically documenting work this way is that when the data or analysis code changes, the results will be updated in the document automatically. This can save hours of fiddly copying and pasting of R output between different programs. Also, if your client wants pages and pages of documented output, **knitr** can provide them with a minimum of typing (e.g., by creating slightly different versions of the same plot over and over again). From a delivery of content perspective, that is certainly an efficiency gain compared with hours of copying and pasting figures!

If your R Markdown documents include time-consuming processing stages, a speed boost can be attained after the first build by setting `opts_chunk$set(cache = TRUE)` in the first chunk of the document. This setting was used to reduce the build times of this book, as can be seen on GitHub (*http://bit.ly/before_scriptR*).

Furthermore, dynamic documents written in R Markdown can compile into a range of output formats including HTML, PDF, and Microsoft's docx. There is a wealth of information on the details of dynamic report writing that is not worth replicating here. Key references are RStudio's excellent website on R Markdown hosted at *rmarkdown.rstudio.com* and, for a more detailed account of dynamic documents with R, *Dynamic Documents with R and Knitr* by Yihui Xie (CRC Press).

R Packages

A strict approach to project management and workflow is treating your projects as R packages. This approach has advantages and limitations. The major risk with treating a project as a package is that the package is quite a strict way of organizing work. Packages are suited for code-intensive projects where code documentation is important. An intermediate approach is to use a *dummy package* that includes a *DESCRIPTION* file in the root directory telling project users which packages must be installed for the code to work. This book is based on a dummy package so that we can easily keep the dependencies up-to-date (see the book's *DESCRIPTION* (*http://bit.ly/effi cientRDESC*) file online for insight into how this works).

Creating packages is good practice in terms of learning to correctly document your code, store example data, and even (via vignettes) ensure reproducibility. But it can take a lot of extra time so should not be taken lightly. This approach to R workflow is appropriate for managing complex projects that repeatedly use the same routines that can be converted into functions. Creating project packages can provide a foundation for generalizing your code for use by others, e.g., via publication on GitHub or CRAN. And R package development has been made much easier in recent years by the development of the **devtools** package, which is highly recommended for anyone attempting to write an R package.

The number of essential elements of R packages differentiates them from other R projects. Three of these are outlined here from an efficiency perspective:

- The *DESCRIPTION* (*http://r-pkgs.had.co.nz/description.html*) file contains key information about the package, including which packages are required for the code contained in your package to work (e.g., using `Imports:`). This is efficient because it means that anyone who installs your package will automatically install the other packages it depends on.

- The *R/* folder contains all the R code that defines your package's functions. Placing your code in a single place and encouraging you to make your code modular in this way can greatly reduce duplication of code on large projects. Furthermore, the documentation of R packages through Roxygen tags (*http://r-pkgs.had.co.nz/man.html#man-workflow*) such as `#' This function does this...` makes it easy for others to use your work. This form of efficient documentation is facilitated by the **roxygen2** package.

- The `data/` folder contains example code for demonstrating to others how the functions work and transporting datasets that will be frequently used in your workflow. Data can be added automatically to your package project using the **devtools** package, with `devtools::use_data()`. This can increase efficiency by providing a way of distributing small-to-medium-sized datasets and making them available when the package is loaded with the function `data("data_set_name")`.

The package **testthat** makes it easier than ever to test your R code as you go, ensuring that nothing breaks. This, combined with *continuous integration* services such as that provided by Travis, makes updating your code base as efficient and robust as possible. This, and more, is described in *Testing R Code* by Richard Cotton (CRC Press).

As with dynamic documents, package development is a large topic. For small *one-off* projects, the time taken in learning how to set up a package may not be worth the savings. However, packages provide a rigorous way of storing code, data, and documentation that can greatly boost productivity in the long run. For more on R packages, see *R Packages* by Hadley Wickham (O'Reilly); the online version (*http://r-pkgs.had.co.nz/*) provides all you need to know about writing R packages for free.

Reference

Berkun, Scott. 2005. *The Art of Project Management*. O'Reilly Media.

Kruchten, Philippe, Robert L Nord, and Ipek Ozkaya. 2012. "Technical Debt: From Metaphor to Theory and Practice." *IEEE Software*, no. 6. IEEE: 18–21.

PMBoK, A. 2000. "Guide to the Project Management Body of Knowledge." *Project Management Institute, Pennsylvania* USA.

Wickham, Hadley. 2015c. *R Packages*. O'Reilly Media.

Eddelbuettel, Dirk, Romain François, J. Allaire, John Chambers, Douglas Bates, and Kevin Ushey. 2011. "Rcpp: Seamless R and C++ Integration." *Journal of Statistical Software* 40 (8): 1–18.

Xie, Yihui. 2015. *Dynamic Documents with R and Knitr*. Vol. 29. CRC Press.

Cotton, Richard. 2016b. *Testing R Code*.

## CHAPTER 5

Efficient Input/Output

This chapter explains how to efficiently read and write data in R. *Input/output* (I/O) is the technical term for reading and writing data: the process of getting information into a particular computer system (in this case, R) and then exporting it to the outside world again (in this case, as a file format that other software can read). Data I/O will be needed on projects where data comes from, or goes to, external sources. However, the majority of R resources and documentation start with the optimistic assumption that your data has already been loaded, ignoring the fact that importing datasets into R and exporting them to the world outside the R ecosystem can be a time-consuming and frustrating process. Tricky, slow, or ultimately unsuccessful data I/O can cripple efficiency right at the outset of a project. Conversely, reading and writing your data efficiently will make your R projects more likely to succeed in the outside world.

The first section introduces **rio**, a *meta package* for efficiently reading and writing data in a range of file formats. **rio** requires only two intuitive functions for data I/O, making it efficient to learn and use. Next, we explore in more detail efficient functions for reading files stored in common plain text file formats from the **readr** and **data.table** packages. Binary formats, which can dramatically reduce file sizes and read/write times, are covered next.

With the accelerating digital revolution and growth in open data, an increasing proportion of the world's data can be downloaded from the internet. This trend is set to continue, making "Getting Data from the Internet" on page 96 on downloading and importing data from the web important for future-proofing your I/O skills. The benchmarks in this chapter demonstrate that choice of file format and packages for data I/O can have a huge impact on computational efficiency.

Before reading in a single line of data, it is worth considering a general principle for reproducible data management: never modify raw data files. Raw data should be seen as read-only, and contain information about its provenance. Keeping the original file name and commenting on its source are a couple of ways to improve reproducibility, even when the data are not publicly available.

Prerequisites

R can read data from a variety of sources. We begin by discussing the generic package **rio** that handles a wide variety of data types. Special attention is paid to CSV files, which leads to the **readr** and **data.table** packages. The relatively new package **feather** is introduced as a binary file format that has cross-language support.

```
library("rio")
library("readr")
library("data.table")
library("feather")
```

We also use the **WDI** package to illustrate accessing online datasets:

```
library("WDI")
```

Top Five Tips for Efficient Data I/O

1. If possible, keep the names of local files downloaded from the internet or copied onto your computer unchanged. This will help you trace the provenance of the data in the future.

2. R's native file format is *.Rds*. These files can be imported and exported using `readRDS()` and `saveRDS()` for fast and space-efficient data storage.

3. Use `import()` from the **rio** package to efficiently import data from a wide range of formats, avoiding the hassle of loading format-specific libraries.

4. Use **readr** or **data.table** equivalents of `read.table()` to efficiently import large text files.

5. Use `file.size()` and `object.size()` to keep track of the size of files and R objects and take action if they get too big.

Versatile Data Import with rio

rio is a veritable multitool for data I/O. **rio** provides easy-to-use and computationally efficient functions for importing and exporting tabular data in a range of file formats. As stated in the package's vignette (*https://cran.r-project.org/web/packages/rio/vignettes/rio.html*), **rio** aims to "simplify the process of importing data into R and exporting data from R." The vignette goes on to to explain how many of the functions for data I/O described in R's Data Import/Export manual (*https://cran.r-*

project.org/doc/manuals/r-release/R-data.html) are outdated (e.g., referring to **WriteXLS** but not the more recent **readxl** package) and difficult to learn.

This is why **rio** is covered at the outset of this chapter: if you just want to get data into R with a minimum of time learning new functions, there is a fair chance that **rio** can help for many common file formats. At the time of writing, these include *.csv*, *.feather*, *.json*, *.dta*, *.xls*, *.xlsx*, and Google Sheets (see the package's Git-Hub page (*https://github.com/leeper/rio*) for up-to-date information). In the following example, we illustrate the key **rio** functions of import() and export():

```
library("rio")
# Specify a file
fname = system.file("extdata/voc_voyages.tsv", package = "efficient")
# Import the file (uses the fread function from data.table)
voyages = import(fname)
# Export the file as an Excel spreadsheet
export(voyages, "voc_voyages.xlsx")
```

There was no need to specify the optional format argument for data import and export functions because this is inferred by the *suffix*, which, in the previous example, is *.tsv* and *.xlsx*, respectively. You can override the inferred file format for both functions with the format argument. You could, for example, create a comma-delimited file called *voc_voyages.xlsx* with export(voyages, "voc_voyages.xlsx", format = "csv"). However, this would not be a good idea because it is important to ensure that a file's suffix matches its format.

To provide another example, the following code chunk downloads and imports as a data frame information about the countries of the world stored in *.json* (downloading data from the internet is covered in more detail in "Getting Data from the Internet" on page 96):

```
caps = import("https://github.com/mledoze/countries/raw/master/countries.json")
```

 The ability to import and use *.json* data is becoming increasingly common as it is a standard output format for many APIs. The **jsonlite** and **geojsonio** packages have been developed to make this as easy as possible.

Exercises

1. The final line in the preceding code chunk shows a neat feature of **rio** and some other packages: the output format is determined by the suffix of the filename, which makes for concise code. Try opening the *voc_voyages.xlsx* file with an editor such as LibreOffice Calc or Microsoft Excel to ensure that the export worked, before removing this rather inefficient file format from your system:

```
file.remove("voc_voyages.xlsx")
```

2. Try saving the the `voyages` data frames into three other file formats of your choosing (see `vignette("rio")` for supported formats). Try opening these in external programs. Which file formats are more portable?

3. As a bonus exercise, create a simple benchmark to compare the write times for the different file formats used to complete the previous exercise. Which is fastest? Which is the most space-efficient?

Plain-Text Formats

Plain-text data files are encoded in a format (typically UTF-8) that can be read by humans and computers alike. The great thing about plain text is its simplicity and ease of use: any programming language can read a plain-text file. The most common plain-text format is *.csv*, comma-separated values, in which columns are separated by commas and rows are separated by line breaks. This is illustrated in the simple example here:

```
Person, Nationality, Country of Birth
Robin, British, England
Colin, British, Scotland
```

There is often more than one way to read data into R, and *.csv* files are no exception. The method you choose has implications for computational efficiency. This section investigates methods for getting plain-text files into R, with a focus on three approaches: base R's plain-text reading functions such as `read.csv()`; the **data.table** approach, which uses the function `fread()`; and the newer **readr** package, which provides `read_csv()` and other `read_*()` functions such as `read_tsv()`. Although these functions perform differently, they are largely cross-compatible, as illustrated in the following code chunk, which loads data on the concentration of CO_2 in the atmosphere over time:

In general, you should never "hand-write" a CSV file. Instead, you should use `write.csv()` or an equivalent function. The Internet Engineering Task Force has the CSV definition (*https://www.ietf.org/rfc/rfc4180.txt*) that facilitates sharing CSV files between tools and operating systems.

```
df_co2 = read.csv("extdata/co2.csv")
df_co2_dt = readr::read_csv("extdata/co2.csv")
#> Warning: Missing column names filled in: 'X1' [1]
#> Parsed with column specification:
#> cols(
#>   X1 = col_integer(),
#>   time = col_double(),
#>   co2 = col_double()
```

```
#> )
df_co2_readr = data.table::fread("extdata/co2.csv")
```

 Note that a function *derived from* another in this context means that it calls another function. The functions such as `read.csv()` and `read.delim()`, in fact, are *wrappers* around `read.table()`. This can be seen in the source code of `read.csv()`, for example, which shows that the function is roughly the equivalent of `read.table(file, header = TRUE, sep = ",")`.

Although this section is focused on reading text files, it demonstrates the wider principle that the speed and flexibility advantages of additional read functions can be offset by the disadvantages of additional package dependency (in terms of complexity and maintaining the code) for small datasets. The real benefits kick in on large datasets. Of course, there are some data types that *require* a certain package to load in R: the **readstata13** package, for example, was developed solely to read in *.dta* files generated by versions of Stata 13 and above.

Figure 5-1 demonstrates that the relative performance gains of the **data.table** and **readr** approaches increase with data size, especially for data with many rows. Below around 1 MB, `read.csv()` is actually *faster* than `read_csv()`, while `fread()` is much faster than both, although these savings are likely to be inconsequential for such smaller datasets.

For files above 100 MB in size, `fread()` and `read_csv()` can be expected to be around *five times faster* than `read.csv()`. This efficiency gain may be inconsequential for a one-off file of 100 MB running on a fast computer (which still takes less than a minute with `read.csv()`), but could represent an important speed-up if you frequently load large text files.

When tested on a large (4 GB) *.csv* file, it was found that `fread()` and `read_csv()` were almost identical in load times and that `read.csv()` took about five times longer. This consumed more than 10 GB of RAM, making it unsuitable to run on many computers (see "Random Access Memory" on page 155 for more on memory). Note that both **readr** and base methods can be made significantly faster by prespecifying the column types at the outset (see the following code chunk). Further details are provided by the help in `?read.table`.

```
read.csv(file_name, colClasses = c("numeric", "numeric"))
```

In some cases with R programming, there is a trade-off between speed and robustness. This is illustrated here with reference to differences in how **readr**, **data.table**, and base R handle unexpected values. Figure 5-1 highlights the benefit of switching to `fread()` and (eventually) to `read_csv()` as the dataset size increases. For a small (1 MB) dataset, `fread()` is about five times faster than base R.

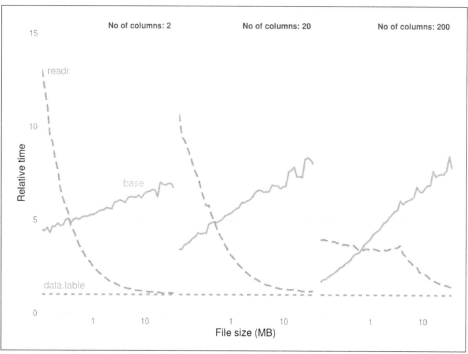

Figure 5-1. Benchmarks of base, data.table, and readr approaches for reading CSV files, using the functions read.csv(), fread(), and read_csv(), respectively. The facets ranging from 2 to 200 represent the number of columns in the CSV file.

Differences Between fread() and read_csv()

The file *voc_voyages* was taken from a dataset on Dutch naval expeditions and used with permission from the CWI Database Architectures Group. The data is described more fully at monetdb.org (*http://bit.ly/monetDBR*). From this dataset, we primarily use the voyages table, which lists Dutch shipping expeditions by their date of departure.

```
fname = system.file("extdata/voc_voyages.tsv", package = "efficient")
voyages_base = read.delim(fname)
```

When we run the equivalent operation using **readr**,

```
voyages_readr = readr::read_tsv(fname)
#> Parsed with column specification:
#> cols(
#>   .default = col_character(),
#>   number = col_integer(),
#>   trip = col_integer(),
#>   tonnage = col_integer(),
#>   departure_date = col_date(format = ""),
#>   cape_arrival = col_date(format = ""),
```

```
#>    cape_departure = col_date(format = ""),
#>    arrival_date = col_date(format = ""),
#>    next_voyage = col_integer()
#> )
#> See spec(...) for full column specifications.
#> Warning: 2 parsing failures.
#>  row            col   expected   actual
#> 4403 cape_arrival   date like   2-01-01
#> 4592 cape_departure date like   8-05-17
```

a warning is raised regarding row 2841 in the built variable. This is because
read_*() decides what class each variable is based on the first 1,000 rows, rather than
all rows, as base read.*() functions do. Printing the offending element:

```
voyages_base$built[2841] # a factor.
#> [1] 1721-01-01
#> 182 Levels:  1 784 1,86 1135 1594 1600 1612 1613 1614 1615 1619 ... taken 1672
voyages_readr$built[2841] # an NA: text cannot be converted to numeric
#> [1] "1721-01-01"
```

Reading the file using **data.table**:

```
# Verbose warnings not shown
voyages_dt = data.table::fread(fname)
```

generates five warning messages stating that columns 2, 4, 9, 10, and 11 were Bumped
to type character on data row ..., with the offending rows printed in place
of .... Instead of changing the offending values to NA, as **readr** does for the built
column (9), fread() automatically converts any columns it considers as numeric into
characters. An additional feature of fread() is that it can read-in a selection of the
columns, either by their index or name, using the select argument. This is illustrated
in the following code by reading in only half (the first 11) columns from the voyages
dataset and comparing the result to using fread() on all columns.

```
microbenchmark(times = 5,
  with_select = data.table::fread(fname, select = 1:11),
  without_select = data.table::fread(fname)
)
#> Unit: milliseconds
#>             expr   min    lq  mean median    uq   max neval
#>      with_select  9.52  9.58  9.68   9.71  9.74  9.86     5
#>   without_select 16.02 16.45 16.57  16.64 16.76 16.98     5
```

To summarize, the differences between base, **readr**, and **data.table** functions for
reading in data go beyond code execution times. The functions read_csv() and
fread() boost speed partially at the expense of robustness because they decide column classes based on a small sample of available data. The similarities and differences
between the approaches are summarized for the Dutch shipping data in Table 5-1.

Table 5-1. Comparison of the classes created by base, readr, and data.table for a selection of variables in the voyages dataset

Packages	number	boatname	built	departure_date
base	integer	factor	factor	factor
readr	integer	character	character	date
data.table	integer	character	character	character

Table 5-1 shows four main similarities and differences between the three types of read functions:

- For uniform data such as the *number* variable in Table 5-1, all reading methods yield the same result (integer, in this case).

- For columns that are obviously characters such as *boatname*, the base method results in factors (unless `stringsAsFactors` is set to `TRUE`), whereas `fread()` and `read_csv()` functions return characters.

- For columns in which the first 1,000 rows are of one type but which contain anomalies, such as *built* and *departure_data* in the shipping example, `fread()` coerces the result to characters. `read_csv()` and siblings, by contrast, keep the class that is correct for the first 1,000 rows and sets the anomalous records to `NA`. This is illustrated in Table 5-1, where `read_tsv()` produces a `numeric` class for the *built* variable, ignoring the nonnumeric text in row 2841.

- `read_*()` functions generate objects of class `tbl_df`, an extension of the `data.frame` class, as discussed in "Efficient Data Processing with dplyr" on page 108. `fread()` generates objects of class `data.table()`. These can be used as standard data frames but differ subtly in their behavior.

An additional difference is that `read_csv()` creates data frames of class `tbl_df` *and* the `data.frame`. This makes no practical difference, unless the **tibble** package is loaded, as described in "Efficient Data Frames with tibble" on page 100 in the next chapter.

The wider point associated with these tests is that functions that save time can also lead to additional considerations or complexities in your workflow. Taking a look at what is going on under the hood of fast functions to increase speed, as we have done in this section, can help you understand the additional consequences of choosing fast functions over slower functions from base R.

Preprocessing Text Outside R

There are circumstances when datasets become too large to read directly into R. Reading in a 4 GB text file using the functions tested previously, for example, consumes all available RAM on a 16 GB machine. To overcome this limitation, external *stream processing* tools can be used to preprocess large text files. The following command, using the Linux command line *shell* (or Windows-based Linux shell emulator Cygwin (*https://cygwin.com/install.html*)) command `split`, for example, will break a large multi-GB file into many 1 GB chunks, each of which is more manageable for R:

```
split -b100m bigfile.csv
```

The result is a series of files, set to 100 MB each, with the `-b100m` argument in the previous code. By default, these will be called `xaa`, `xab` and could be read in *one chunk at a time* (e.g., using `read.csv()`, `fread()`, or `read_csv()`, described in the previous section) without crashing most modern computers.

Splitting a large file into individual chunks may allow it to be read into R. This is not an efficient way to import large datasets, however, because it results in a nonrandom sample of the data this way. A more efficient, robust, and scalable way to work with large datasets is via databases, covered in "Working with Databases" on page 119 in the next chapter.

Binary File Formats

There are limitations to plain-text files. Even the trusty CSV format is "restricted to tabular data, lacks type-safety, and has limited precision for numeric values" (Eddelbuettel, Stokely, and Ooms 2016). Once you have read in the raw data (e.g., from a plain-text file) and tidied it (covered in the next chapter), it is common to want to save it for future use. Saving it after tidying is recommended to reduce the chance of having to run all the data-cleaning code again. We recommend saving tidied versions of large datasets in one of the binary formats covered in this section as this will decrease read/write times and file sizes, making your data more portable.[1]

Unlike plain-text files, data stored in binary formats cannot be read by humans. This allows space-efficient data compression, but means that the files will be less language-agnostic. R's native file format, *.Rds*, for example, may be difficult to read and write using external programs such as Python or LibreOffice Calc. This section provides an overview of binary file formats in R, with benchmarks to show how they compare with the plain-text format *.csv* covered in the previous section.

---

1 Geographical data, for example, can be slow to read in external formats. A large *.shp* or *.geojson* file can take more than 100 times longer to load than an equivalent *.Rds* or *.Rdata* file.

Native Binary Formats: Rdata or Rds?

.Rds and *.RData* are R's native binary file formats. These formats are optimized for speed and compression ratios. But what is the difference between them? The following code chunk demonstrates the key difference between them:

```
save(df_co2, file = "extdata/co2.RData")
saveRDS(df_co2, "extdata/co2.Rds")
load("extdata/co2.RData")
df_co2_rds = readRDS("extdata/co2.Rds")
identical(df_co2, df_co2_rds)
#> [1] TRUE
```

The first method is the most widely used. It uses the `save()` function, which takes any number of R objects and writes them to a file, which must be specified by the `file =` argument. `save()` is like `save.image()`, which saves *all* the objects currently loaded in R.

The second method is slightly less used, but we recommend it. Apart from being slightly more concise for saving single R objects, the `readRDS()` function is more flexible; as shown in the subsequent line, the resulting object can be assigned to any name. In this case, we called it `df_co2_rds` (which we show to be identical to `df_co2`, loaded with the `load()` command), but we could have called it anything or simply printed it to the console.

Using `saveRDS()` is good practice because it forces you to specify object names. If you use `save()` without care, you could forget the names of the objects you saved and accidentally overwrite objects that already exist.

The Feather File Format

Feather was developed as a collaboration between R and Python developers to create a fast, light, and language-agnostic format for storing data frames. The following code chunk shows how it can be used to save and then reload the `df_co2` dataset loaded previously in both R and Python:

```
library("feather")
write_feather(df_co2, "extdata/co2.feather")
df_co2_feather = read_feather("extdata/co2.feather")

import feather
import feather
path = 'data/co2.feather'
df_co2_feather = feather.read_dataframe(path)
```

Benchmarking Binary File Formats

We know that binary formats are advantageous from space and read/write time perspectives, but how much so? The benchmarks in this section, based on large matrices containing random numbers, are designed to help answer this question. Figure 5-2 shows that the *relative* efficiency gains of feather and Rds formats, compared with base CSV. From left to right, Figure 5-2 shows benefits in terms of file size, read times, and write times.

In terms of write times, Rds files perform the best, occupying just over a quarter of the hard disk space compared with the equivalent CSV files. The equivalent feather format also outperformed the CSV format, occupying around half the disk space.

The results of this simple disk usage benchmark show that saving data in a compressed binary format can save space and, if your data will be shared online, data download time and bandwidth usage perspectives. But how does each method compare from a computational efficiency perceptive? The read and write times for each file format are illustrated in the middle and right-hand panels of Figure 5-2.

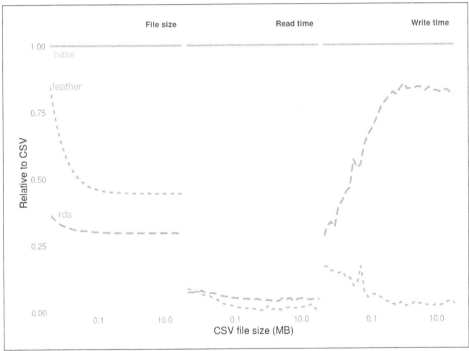

Figure 5-2. Comparison of the performance of binary formats for reading and writing datasets with 20 columns with the plain-text format CSV; the functions used to read the files were read.csv(), readRDS(), and feather::read_feather(), respectively. The functions used to write the files were write.csv(), saveRDS(), and feather::write_feather().

The results show that file size is not a reliable predictor of data read and write times. This is due to the computational overheads of compression. Although feather files occupied more disk space, they were roughly equivalent in terms of read times: the functions `read_feather()` and `readRDS()` were consistently around 10 times faster than `read.csv()`. In terms of write times, feather excels: `write_feather()` was around 10 times faster than `write.csv()`, whereas `saveRDS()` was only around 1.2 times faster.

 Note that the performance of different file formats depends on the content of the data being saved. The benchmarks here showed savings for matrices of random numbers. For real-life data, the results would be quite different. The voyages dataset, saved as an Rds file, occupied less than a quarter the disk space as the original TSV file, whereas the file size was larger than the original when saved as a feather file!

Protocol Buffers

Google's Protocol Buffers (*https://developers.google.com/protocol-buffers/*) offer a portable, efficient, and scalable solution to binary data storage. A recent package, **RProtoBuf**, provides an R interface. This approach is not covered in this book, as it is new, advanced, and not (at the time of writing) widely used in the R community. The approach is discussed in detail in a paper (*http://bit.ly/RProtoBufapproach*) on the subject, which also provides an excellent overview of the issues associated with different file formats (Eddelbuettel, Stokely, and Ooms 2016).

Getting Data from the Internet

The following code chunk shows how the functions `download.file`[2] and `unzip` can be used to download and unzip a dataset from the internet. R can automate processes that are often performed manually (e.g., through the graphical user interface of a web browser) with potential advantages for reproducibility and programmer efficiency. The result is data stored neatly in the `data` directory ready to be imported. Note that we deliberately kept the filename intact to help with documentation, enhancing understanding of the data's *provenance*, so future users can quickly find out where the data came from. Note also that part of the dataset is stored in the **efficient** package. Using R for basic file management can help create a reproducible workflow, as illustrated here:

```
url = "https://www.monetdb.org/sites/default/files/voc_tsvs.zip"
download.file(url, "voc_tsvs.zip") # download file
unzip("voc_tsvs.zip", exdir = "data") # unzip files
file.remove("voc_tsvs.zip") # tidy up by removing the zip file
```

---

2 Since R 3.2.3 the base function `download.file()` can be used to download from secure (*https://*) connections on any operating system.

This workflow equally applies to downloading and loading single files. Note that one could make the code more concise by replacing the second line with df = read.csv(url). However, we recommend downloading the file to disk so that if for some reason it fails (e.g., if you would like to skip the first few lines), you don't have to keep downloading the file over and over again. The following code downloads and loads data on atmospheric concentrations of CO_2. Note that this dataset is also available from the **datasets** package.

```
url = "https://vincentarelbundock.github.io/Rdatasets/csv/datasets/co2.csv"
download.file(url, "extdata/co2.csv")
df_co2 = read_csv("extdata/co2.csv")
```

There are now many R packages to assist with the download and import of data. The organization rOpenSci (*https://ropensci.org/*) supports a number of these. The following example illustrates this using the WDI package (not supported by rOpenSci) to accesses World Bank data on CO_2 emissions in the transport sector:

```
library("WDI")
WDIsearch("CO2") # search for data on a topic
co2_transport = WDI(indicator = "EN.CO2.TRAN.ZS") # import data
```

There will be situations where you cannot download the data directly or when the data cannot be made available. In this case, simply providing a comment relating to the data's origin (e.g., # Downloaded from http://example.com) before referring to the dataset can greatly improve the utility of the code to yourself and others.

There are a number of R packages that provide more advanced functionality than simply downloading files. The CRAN task view on web technologies (*https://cran.r-project.org/web/views/WebTechnologies.html*) provides a comprehensive list. The two packages for interacting with web pages are **httr** and **RCurl**. The former package provides (a relatively) user-friendly interface for executing standard HTTP methods such as GET and POST. It also provides support for web authentication protocols and returns HTTP status codes that are essential for debugging. The **RCurl** package focuses on lower-level support and is particularly useful for web-based XML support or FTP operations.

Accessing Data Stored in Packages

Most well-documented packages provide some example data for you to play with. This can help demonstrate use cases in specific domains that use a particular data format. The command data(package = "package_name") will show the datasets in a package. Datasets provided by **dplyr**, for example, can be viewed with data(package = "dplyr").

Raw data (i.e., data that has not been converted into R's native *.Rds* format) is usually located within the subfolder *extdata* in R, which corresponds to *inst/extdata* when developing packages. The function `system.file()` outputs file paths associated with specific packages. To see all the external files within the **readr** package, for example, you could use the following command:

```
list.files(system.file("extdata", package = "readr"))
#> [1] "challenge.csv"    "compound.log"     "epa78.txt"
#> [4] "example.log"      "fwf-sample.txt"   "massey-rating.txt"
#> [7] "mtcars.csv"       "mtcars.csv.bz2"   "mtcars.csv.zip"
```

Further, to *look around* to see what files are stored in a particular package, you could type the following, taking advantage of RStudio's intellisense file completion capabilities (using copy and paste to enter the file path):

```
system.file(package = "readr")
#> [1] "/home/robin/R/x86_64-pc-linux-gnu-library/3.3/readr"
```

Hitting Tab after the second command should trigger RStudio to create a miniature pop-up box listing the files within the folder, as illustrated in Figure 5-3.

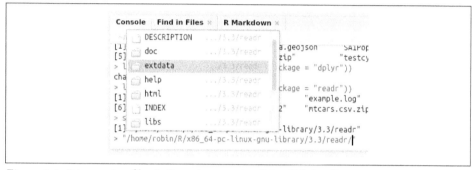

Figure 5-3. Discovering files in R packages using RStudio's intellisense

References

Eddelbuettel, Dirk, Murray Stokely, and Jeroen Ooms. 2016. "RProtoBuf: Efficient Cross-Language Data Serialization in R." *Journal of Statistical Software* 71 (1): 1–24. doi:10.18637/jss.v071.i02 (*http://bit.ly/RProtoBufapproach*).

## CHAPTER 6

Efficient Data Carpentry

There are many words for data processing. You can clean, hack, manipulate, munge, refine, and tidy your dataset, ready for the next stage. Each word says something about perceptions that people have about the process: data processing is often seen as dirty work, an unpleasant necessity that must be endured before the real fun and important work begins. This perception is wrong. Getting your data ship-shape is a respectable and in some cases vital skill. For this reason, we use the more admirable term *data carpentry*.

This metaphor is not accidental. Carpentry is the process of taking rough pieces of wood and working with care, diligence, and precision to create a finished product. A carpenter does not hack at the wood at random. He or she will inspect the raw material and select the right tool for the job. In the same way, *data carpentry* is the process of taking rough, raw, and to some extent randomly arranged input data and creating neatly organized and *tidy* data. Learning the skill of data carpentry early will yield benefits for years to come. "Give me six hours to chop down a tree and I will spend the first four sharpening the axe," as the saying goes.

Data processing is a critical stage in any project involving datasets from external sources (i.e., most real-world applications). In the same way that technical debt, discussed in Chapter 5, can cripple your workflow, working with messy data can lead to project management hell.

Fortunately, done efficiently, at the outset of your project (rather than halfway through when it may be too late) and using appropriate tools, this data processing stage can be highly rewarding. More importantly, from an efficiency perspective, working with clean data will be beneficial for every subsequent stage of your R project. So, for data-intensive applications, this could be the most important chapter in this book. In it, we cover the following topics:

- Tidying data with **tidyr**
- Processing data with **dplyr**
- Working with databases
- Data processing with **data.table**

Prerequisites

This chapter relies on a number of packages for data cleaning and processing. Check that they are installed on your computer and load them with:

```
library("tibble")
library("tidyr")
library("stringr")
library("readr")
library("dplyr")
library("data.table")
```

RSQLite and **ggmap** are also used in a couple of examples, though they are not central to the chapter's content.

Top Five Tips for Efficient Data Carpentry

1. Time spent preparing your data at the beginning can save hours of frustration in the long run.
2. *Tidy data* provides a concept for organizing data, and the package **tidyr** provides some functions for this work.
3. The data_frame class defined by the **tibble** package makes datasets efficient to print and easy to work with.
4. **dplyr** provides fast and intuitive data processing functions; **data.table** has unmatched speed for some data processing applications.
5. The %>% pipe operator can help clarify complex data processing workflows.

Efficient Data Frames with tibble

tibble is a package that defines a new data frame class for R, the tbl_df. These *tibble diffs* (as their inventor suggests (*https://github.com/hadley/tibble*) they should be pronounced) are like the base class data.frame but with more user-friendly printing, subsetting, and factor handling.

A tibble data frame is an S3 object with three classes, tbl_df, tbl, and data.frame. Since the object has the data.frame tag, this means that if a tbl_df or tbl method isn't available, the object will be passed on to the appropriate data.frame function.

To create a **tibble** data frame, we use the tibble function:

```
library("tibble")
tibble(x = 1:3, y = c("A", "B", "C"))
#> # A tibble: 3 × 2
#>       x     y
#>   <int> <chr>
#> 1     1     A
#> 2     2     B
#> 3     3     C
```

The previous example illustrates the main differences between the **tibble** and base R approaches to data frames:

- When printed, the **tibble** diff reports the class of each variable. data.frame objects do not.

- Character vectors are not coerced into factors when they are incorporated into a tbl_df, as can be seen by the <chr> heading between the variable name and the second column. By contrast, data.frame() coerces characters into factors, which can cause problems further down the line.

- When printing a **tibble** diff to screen, only the first 10 rows are displayed. The number of columns printed depends on the window size.

Other differences can be found in the associated help page: help("tibble").

You can create a **tibble** data frame row by row using the tribble() function.

Exercise

1. Create the following data frame:

   ```
   df_base = data.frame(colA = "A")
   ```

   Try and guess the output of the following commands:

   ```
   print(df_base)
   df_base$colA
   df_base$col
   df_base$colB
   ```

Now create a **tibble** data frame and repeat the preceding commands.

Tidying Data with tidyr and Regular Expressions

A key skill in data analysis is understanding the structure of datasets and being able to *reshape* them. This is important from a workflow efficiency perspective: more than half of a data analyst's time can be spent reformatting datasets (Wickham 2014b), so getting it into a suitable form early could save hours in the future. Converting data into a *tidy* form is also advantageous from a computational efficiency perspective because it is usually faster to run analysis and plotting commands on tidy data.

Data tidying includes data cleaning and data reshaping. Data cleaning is the process of reformatting and labeling messy data. Packages including **stringi** and **stringr** can help update messy character strings using regular expressions; **assertive** and **assertr** packages can perform diagnostic checks for data integrity at the outset of a data analysis project. A common data-cleaning task is the conversion of nonstandard text strings into date formats as described in the **lubridate** vignette (see `vignette("lubridate")`). Tidying is a broader concept, however, and also includes reshaping data so that it is in a form more conducive to data analysis and modeling. The process of reshaping is illustrated by Tables 6-1 and 6-2, provided by Hadley Wickham and loaded using the following code:

```
library("efficient")
data(pew) # see ?pew - dataset from the efficient package
pew[1:3, 1:4] # take a look at the data
#> # A tibble: 3 × 4
#>    religion `<$10k` `$10--20k` `$20--30k`
#>      <chr>   <int>     <int>      <int>
#> 1 Agnostic     27        34         60
#> 2  Atheist     12        27         37
#> 3 Buddhist     27        21         30
```

Tables 6-1 and 6-2 show a subset of the *wide* pew and *long* (tidy) pewt datasets, respectively. They have different dimensions, but they contain precisely the same information. Column names in the *wide* form in Table 6-1 became a new variable in the *long* form in Table 6-2. According to the concept of *tidy data*, the long form is correct. Note that *correct* here is used in the context of data analysis and graphical visualization. Because R is a vector-based language, tidy data also has an efficiency advantage: it's often faster to operate on a few long columns than several short ones. Furthermore, the powerful and efficient packages **dplyr** and **ggplot2** were designed around tidy data. Wide data, however, can be space efficient, and is common for presentation in summary tables, so it's useful to be able to transfer between wide (or otherwise *untidy*) and tidy formats.

Tidy data has the following characteristics (Wickham 2014b):

- Each variable forms a column.
- Each observation forms a row.
- Each type of observational unit forms a table.

Because there is only one observational unit in the example (religions), it can be described in a single table. Large and complex datasets are usually represented by multiple tables, with unique identifiers or *keys* to join them together (Codd 1979).

Two common operations facilitated by **tidyr** are *gathering* and *splitting* columns.

Make Wide Tables Long with gather()

Gathering means making *wide* tables *long* by converting column names to a new variable. This is done with the function `gather()` (the inverse of which is `spread()`). The process is illustrated in Tables 6-1 and 6-2. The code that performs this operation is provided in the following code block. This converts a table with 18 rows and 10 columns into a tidy dataset with 162 rows and 3 columns (compare the output with the output of `pew`, shown previously):

```
dim(pew)
#> [1] 18 10
pewt = gather(data = pew, key = Income, value = Count, -religion)
dim(pewt)
#> [1] 162    3
pewt[c(1:3, 50),]
#> # A tibble: 4 × 3
#>   religion  Income Count
#>      <chr>    <chr> <int>
#> 1 Agnostic   <$10k    27
#> 2  Atheist   <$10k    12
#> 3 Buddhist   <$10k    27
#> 4 Orthodox $20--30k    23
```

The previous code demonstrates the three arguments that `gather()` requires:

1. `data`, a data frame in which column names will become row values.
2. `key`, the name of the categorical variable into which the column names in the original datasets are converted.
3. `value`, the name of cell value columns.

As with other functions in the *tidyverse*, all arguments are given using bare names, rather than character strings. Arguments 2 and 3 can be specified by the user, and have no relation to the existing data. Furthermore, an additional argument, set as `-religion`, was used to remove the religion variable from the gathering, ensuring that the values in these columns are the first column in the output. If no `-religion` argument is specified, all column names are used in the key, meaning the results simply report all 180 column/value pairs resulting from the input dataset with 10 columns by 18 rows:

```
gather(pew)
#> # A tibble: 180 × 2
#>       key    value
#>     <chr>    <chr>
#> 1 religion Agnostic
#> 2 religion  Atheist
#> 3 religion Buddhist
#> 4 religion Catholic
#> # ... with 176 more rows
```

Table 6-1. First six rows of the aggregated Pew dataset from Wickham (2014a) in an untidy form

Religion	<$10k	$10–20k	$20–30k
Agnostic	27	34	60
Atheist	12	27	37
Buddhist	27	21	30

Table 6-2. Long form of the Pew dataset represented in the previous table showing the minimum values for annual incomes (includes part-time work)

Religion	Income	Count
Agnostic	<$10k	27
Atheist	<$10k	12
Buddhist	<$10k	27
Agnostic	$10–20k	34
Atheist	$10–20k	27
Buddhist	$10–20k	21
Agnostic	$20–30k	60
Atheist	$20–30k	37
Buddhist	$20–30k	30

Split Joint Variables with separate()

Splitting means taking a variable that is really two variables combined and creating two separate columns from it. A classic example is age-sex variables (e.g., `m0-10` and `f0-10` to represent males and females in the 0 to 10 age band). Splitting such variables can be done with the `separate()` function, as illustrated in Tables 6-3 and 6-4 and in the following code chunk. See `?separate` for more information on this function.

```
agesex = c("m0-10", "f0-10") # create compound variable
n = c(3, 5) # create a value for each observation
agesex_df = tibble(agesex, n) # create a data frame
separate(agesex_df, col = agesex, into = c("age", "sex"))
#> # A tibble: 2 × 3
#>     age   sex     n
#> * <chr> <chr> <dbl>
#> 1    m0    10     3
#> 2    f0    10     5
```

Table 6-3. Joined age and sex variables in one column

agesex	n
m0-10	3
f0-10	5

Table 6-4. Age and sex variables separated by the function separate

sex	age	n
m	0-10	3
f	0-10	5

Other tidyr Functions

There are other tidying operations that **tidyr** can perform, as described in the package's vignette (`vignette("tidy-data")`). The wider issue of manipulation is a large topic with major potential implications for efficiency (Spector 2008) and this section only covers some of the key operations. More important is understanding the principles behind converting messy data into standard output forms.

These same principles can also be applied to the representation of model results. The **broom** package provides a standard output format for model results, easing interpretation (see the broom vignette (*http://bit.ly/broomvignette*)). The function `broom::tidy()` can be applied to a wide range of model objects and return the model's output in a standardized data frame output.

Usually, it is more efficient to use the nonstandard evaluation version of variable names, as these can be autocompleted by RStudio. In some cases, you may want to use standard evaluation and refer to variable names using quotation marks. To do this, _ can be added to **dplyr** and **tidyr** function names to allow the use of standard evaluation. Thus the standard evaluation version of `separate(agesex_df, agesex, c("sex", "age"), 1)` is `separate_(agesex_df, "agesex", c("sex", "age"), 1)`.

Regular Expressions

Regular expressions (commonly known as *regex*) is a language for describing and manipulating text strings. There are books on the subject, and several good tutorials on regex in R, such as *Handling and Processing Strings in R* by Gaston Sanchez (Trowchez Editions), so we'll just scratch the surface of the topic, and provide a taste of what is possible. Regex is a deep topic. However, knowing the basics can save a huge amount of time from a data-tidying perspective, by automating the cleaning of messy strings.

In this section, we teach both **stringr** and base R ways of doing pattern matching. The former provides easy-to-remember function names and consistency. The latter is useful to know as you'll find lots of base R regex code in other people's code because **stringr** is relatively new and not installed by default. The foundational regex operation is to detect whether a particular text string exists in an element, which is done with grepl() and str_detect() in base R and **stringr**, respectively:

```
library("stringr")
x = c("Hi I'm Robin.", "DoB 1985")

grepl(pattern = "9", x = x)
#> [1] FALSE  TRUE
str_detect(string = x, pattern = "9")
#> [1] FALSE  TRUE
```

 stringr does not include a direct replacement for grep(). You can use which(str_detect()) instead.

Notice that str_detect() begins with str_. This is a common feature of all **stringr** functions. This can be efficient because if you want to do some regex work, you just need to type str_ and then press the Tab key to see a list of all the options. The various base R regex function names, by contrast, are hard to remember, including regmatches(), strsplit(), and gsub(). The **stringr** equivalents have more intuitive names that relate to the intention of the functions: str_match_all(), str_split(), and str_replace_all(), respectively.

There is more to say on the topic, but rather than repeat what has been said elsewhere, we feel it is more efficient to direct the interested reader toward existing excellent resources for learning regex in R. We recommend reading, in order:

- The Strings chapter (*http://r4ds.had.co.nz/strings.html*) of *R for Data Science* by Grolemund and Wickham (O'Reilly)
- The **stringr** vignette (vignette("stringr"))

- The detailed tutorial on regex in base R (Sanchez 2013)
- For more advanced topics, reading the documentation and online articles (*http://www.rexamine.com/blog/*) about the **stringi** package, on which **stringr** depends

Exercises

1. What are the three criteria of tidy data?

2. Load and look at subsets of these datasets. The first is the Pew datasets we've been using already. The second reports the points that define, roughly, the geographical boundaries of different London boroughs. What is *untidy* about each?

```
head(pew, 10)
#> # A tibble: 10 × 10
#>    religion <$10k $10-20k $20-30k $30-40k $40-50k $50-75
#>       <chr> <int>   <int>   <int>   <int>   <int>  <int>
#> 1 Agnostic    27      34      60      81      76    137
#> 2  Atheist    12      27      37      52      35     70
#> 3 Buddhist    27      21      30      34      33     58
#> 4 Catholic   418     617     732     670     638   1116
#> # ... with 6 more rows, and 3 more variables: `$75--100k` <int>,
#> #   `$100--150k` <int>, `>150k` <int>
data(lnd_geo_df)
head(lnd_geo_df, 10)
#>                  name_date population      x      y
#> 1                Bromley-2001     295535 544362 172379
#> 2                Bromley-2001     295535 549546 169911
#> 3                Bromley-2001     295535 539596 160796
#> 4                Bromley-2001     295535 533693 170730
#> 5                Bromley-2001     295535 533718 170814
#> 6                Bromley-2001     295535 534004 171442
#> 7                Bromley-2001     295535 541105 173356
#> 8                Bromley-2001     295535 544362 172379
#> 9   Richmond upon Thames-2001     172330 523605 176321
#> 10  Richmond upon Thames-2001     172330 521455 172362
```

3. Convert each of the preceding datasets into tidy form.

4. Consider the following string of phone numbers and fruits from "Stringr: Modern, Consistent String Processing" by Hadley Wickham (*The R Journal*):

```
strings = c("219 733 8965", "329-293-8753 ", "banana", "595 794 7569",
            "387 287 6718", "apple", "233.398.9187 ",
            "482 952 3315", "239 923 8115", "842 566 4692",
            "Work: 579-499-7527", "$1000", "Home: 543.355.3679")
```

Write functions in **stringr** and base R that return:

- A logical vector reporting whether or not each string contains a number

- Complete words only, without extraneous nonletter characters

```
str_detect(string = strings, pattern = "[0-9]")
#>  [1]  TRUE  TRUE FALSE  TRUE  TRUE FALSE  TRUE  TRUE  TRUE  TRUE
#> [12]  TRUE  TRUE
str_extract(strings, pattern = "[A-z]+")
#>  [1] NA        NA        "banana" NA        NA        "apple" NA
#>  [8] NA        NA        NA        "Work"    NA        "Home"
```

Efficient Data Processing with dplyr

After tidying your data, the next stage is typically data processing. This includes the creation of new data, such as a new column that is some function of existing columns, or data analysis, the process of asking directed questions of the data and exporting the results in a user-readable form.

Following the advice in "Package Selection" on page 76, we have carefully selected an appropriate package for these tasks: **dplyr**, which roughly means *data frame pliers*. **dplyr** has a number of advantages over base R and **data.table** approaches to data processing:

- **dplyr** is fast to run (due to its C++ backend) and intuitive to type.
- **dplyr** works well with tidy data, as described previously.
- **dplyr** works well with databases, providing efficiency gains on large datasets.

Furthermore, **dplyr** is efficient to *learn* (see Chapter 10). It has a small number of intuitively named functions, or *verbs*. These were partly inspired by SQL, one of the longest established languages for data analysis, which combines multiple simple functions (such as SELECT and WHERE, roughly analogous to dplyr::select() and dplyr::filter()) to create powerful analysis workflows. Likewise, **dplyr** functions were designed to be used together to solve a wide range of data processing challenges (see Table 6-5).

Table 6-5. dplyr verb functions

dplyr function(s)	Description	Base R functions
filter(), slice()	Subset rows by attribute (filter) or position (slice)	subset(), [
arrange()	Return data ordered by variable(s)	order()
select()	Subset columns	subset(), [, [[
rename()	Rename columns	colnames()
distinct()	Return unique rows	!duplicated()
mutate()	Create new variables (transmute drops existing variables)	transform(), [[

dplyr function(s)	Description	Base R functions
summarize()	Collapse data into a single row	aggregate(), tapply()
sample_n()	Return a sample of the data	sample()

Unlike the base R analogues, **dplyr**'s data processing functions work in a consistent way. Each function takes a data frame object as its first argument and creates another data frame. Variables can be called directly without using the $ operator. **dplyr** was designed to be used with the pipe operator %>% provided by the **magrittr** package, allowing each data processing stage to be represented as a new line. This is illustrated in the following code chunk, which loads a tidy country-level dataset of greenhouse gas emissions from the **efficient** package, and then identifies the countries with the greatest absolute growth in emissions from 1971 to 2012:

```
library("dplyr")
data("ghg_ems", package = "efficient")
top_table =
  ghg_ems %>%
  filter(!grepl("World|Europe", Country)) %>%
  group_by(Country) %>%
  summarize(Mean = mean(Transportation),
            Growth = diff(range(Transportation))) %>%
  top_n(3, Growth) %>%
  arrange(desc(Growth))
```

The results, illustrated in Table 6-6, show that the US has the highest growth and average emissions from the transport sector, followed closely by China. The aim of this code chunk is not for you to somehow read it and understand it; it is to provide a taster of **dplyr**'s unique syntax, which is described in more detail throughout the duration of this section.

Table 6-6. The top three countries in terms of average CO_2 emissions from transport since 1971, and growth in transport emissions over that period ($MTCO_2e/yr$)

Country	Mean	Growth
United States	1462	709
China	214	656
India	85	170

Building on the *learning by doing* ethic, the remainder of this section works through these functions to process and begin to analyze a dataset on economic equality provided by the World Bank. The input dataset can be loaded as follows:

```
# Load global inequality data
data(wb_ineq)
```

dplyr is a large package and can be seen as a language in its own right. Following the *walk before you run* principle, we'll start simply, by filtering and aggregating rows.

Renaming Columns

Renaming data columns is a common task that can make writing code faster by using short, intuitive names. The **dplyr** function rename() makes this easy.

Note that in this code block the variable name is surrounded by back-quotes (`). This allows R to refer to column names that are nonstandard. Note also the syntax: rename takes the data frame as the first object and then creates new variables by specifying new_variable_name = original_name.

```
library("dplyr")
wb_ineq = rename(wb_ineq, code = `Country Code`)
```

To rename multiple columns, the variable names are simply separated by commas. The base R and **dplyr** way of doing this is illustrated in an older version of the dataset (not run) to show how long, clunky, and inefficient names can be converted into short and lean ones.

```
# The dplyr way (rename two variables)
wb_ineq = rename(wb_ineq,
 top10 = `Income share held by highest 10% [SI.DST.10TH.10]`,
 bot10 = `Income share held by lowest 10% [SI.DST.FRST.10]`)
# The base R way (rename five variables)
names(wb_ineq)[5:9] = c("top10", "bot10", "gini", "b40_cons", "gdp_percap")
```

Changing Column Classes

The *class* of R objects is critical to performance. If a class is incorrectly specified (e.g., if numbers are treated as factors or characters), this will lead to incorrect results. The class of all columns in a data frame can be queried using the function str() (short for display the *str*ucture of an object), as illustrated in the following code, with the inequality data loaded previously.[1]

```
vapply(wb_ineq, class, character(1))
#>      Country         code         Year    Year Code       top10       bot10
#> "character" "character"    "integer" "character"   "numeric"   "numeric"
#>         gini     b40_cons  gdp_percap
#>    "numeric"    "numeric"   "numeric"
```

This shows that although we loaded the data correctly, all columns are seen by R as characters. This means we cannot perform numerical calculations on the dataset: mean(wb_ineq$gini) fails.

Visual inspection of the data (e.g., via View(wb_ineq)) clearly shows that all columns except for 1 to 4 (Country, Country Code, Year, and Year Code) should be numeric. We can reassign the classes of the numeric variables one by one:

---

1 str(wb_ineq) is another way to see the contents of an object, but produces more verbose output.

```
wb_ineq$gini = as.numeric(wb_ineq$gini)
mean(wb_ineq$gini, na.rm = TRUE) # now the mean is calculated
#> [1] 40.5
```

However, the purpose of programming languages is to *automate* tasks and reduce typing. The following code chunk reclassifies all of the numeric variables using data.matrix(), which converts the data frame to a numeric matrix:

```
cols_to_change= 5:9 # column ids to change
wb_ineq[cols_to_change] = data.matrix(wb_ineq[cols_to_change])
vapply(wb_ineq, class, character(1))
#>      Country         code        Year    Year Code       top10        bot10
#> "character" "character"    "integer" "character"   "numeric"    "numeric"
#>         gini       b40_cons  gdp_percap
#>    "numeric"     "numeric"   "numeric"
```

As is so often the case with R, there are many ways to solve the problem. The following code is a one-liner using unlist(), which converts list objects into vectors:

```
wb_ineq[cols_to_change] = as.numeric(unlist(wb_ineq[cols_to_change]))
```

Another one-liner to achieve the same result uses **dplyr**'s mutate_each function:

```
wb_ineq = mutate_each(wb_ineq, "as.numeric", cols_to_change)
```

As with other operations, there are other ways of achieving the same result in R, including the use of loops via apply() and for(). These are shown in the chapter's source code (*https://github.com/csgillespie/efficientR*).

Filtering Rows

dplyr offers an alternative way of filtering data, using filter().

```
# Base R: wb_ineq[wb_ineq$Country == "Australia",]
aus2 = filter(wb_ineq, Country == "Australia")
```

filter() is slightly more flexible than [: filter(wb_ineq, code == "AUS", Year == 1974), works as well as filter(wb_ineq, code == "AUS" & Year == 1974), and takes any number of conditions (see ?filter). filter() is slightly faster than base R.[2] By avoiding the $ symbol, **dplyr** makes subsetting code concise and consistent with other **dplyr** functions. The first argument is a data frame and subsequent raw variable names can be treated as vector objects, which are a defining feature of **dplyr**. In the next section, we'll learn how this syntax can be used alongside the %>% pipe command to write clear data manipulation commands.

---

2 Note that filter is also the name of a function used in the base **stats** library. Typically, packages avoid using names already taken in base R, but this is an exception.

There are **dplyr** equivalents of many base R functions, but these usually work slightly different. The **dplyr** equivalent of aggregate, for example, is to use the grouping function group_by in combination with the general-purpose function summarize (not to be confused with summary in base R), as we shall see in "Data Aggregation" on page 114.

Chaining Operations

Another interesting feature of **dplyr** is its ability to chain operations together. This overcomes one of the aesthetic issues with R code: you can end up with very long commands with many functions nested inside one another to answer relatively simple questions. Combined with the group_by() function, pipes can help condense thousands of lines of data into something human-readable. Here's how you could use the chains to summarize average Gini indexes per decade, for example:

```
wb_ineq %>%
  select(Year, gini) %>%
  mutate(decade = floor(Year / 10) * 10) %>%
  group_by(decade) %>%
  summarize(mean(gini, na.rm = TRUE))
#> # A tibble: 6 × 2
#>   decade `mean(gini, na.rm = TRUE)`
#>    <dbl>                      <dbl>
#> 1   1970                       40.1
#> 2   1980                       37.8
#> 3   1990                       42.0
#> 4   2000                       40.5
#> # ... with 2 more rows
```

Often the best way to learn is to try and break something, so try running the preceding commands with different **dplyr** verbs. By way of explanation, this is what happened:

1. Only the columns Year and gini were selected, using select().

2. A new variable, decade, was created (e.g., 1989 becomes 1980).

3. This new variable was used to group rows in the data frame with the same decade.

4. The mean value per decade was calculated, illustrating how average income inequality was greatest in 1992 but has since decreased slightly.

Let's ask another question to see how **dplyr** chaining workflow can be used to answer questions interactively: what are the five most unequal years for countries containing the letter g? Here's how chains can help organize the analysis needed to answer this question step by step:

```
wb_ineq %>%
  filter(grepl("g", Country)) %>%
  group_by(Year) %>%
  summarize(gini = mean(gini, na.rm  = TRUE)) %>%
  arrange(desc(gini)) %>%
  top_n(n = 5)
#> Selecting by gini
#> # A tibble: 5 × 2
#>    Year  gini
#>   <int> <dbl>
#> 1 1980  46.9
#> 2 1993  46.0
#> 3 2013  44.5
#> 4 1981  43.6
#> # ... with 1 more rows
```

The preceding function consists of six stages, each of which corresponds to a new line and **dplyr** function:

1. Filter out the countries we're interested in (any selection criteria could be used in place of grepl("g", Country)).
2. Group the output by year.
3. Summarize, for each year, the mean Gini index.
4. Arrange the results by average Gini index.
5. Select only the top five most unequal years.

To see why this method is preferable to the nested function approach, take a look at the latter. Even after indenting properly, it looks terrible and is almost impossible to understand!

```
top_n(
  arrange(
    summarize(
      group_by(
        filter(wb_ineq, grepl("g", Country)),
        Year),
      gini = mean(gini, na.rm  = TRUE)),
    desc(gini)),
  n = 5)
```

This section has provided only a taste of what is possible with **dplyr** and why it makes sense from code-writing and computational-efficiency perspectives. For a more detailed account of data processing with R using this approach, we recommend *R for Data Science* by Grolemund and Wickham (O'Reilly).

Exercises

1. Try running each of the preceding chaining examples line by line, so the first two entries for the first example look like this:

```
wb_ineq
#> # A tibble: 6,925 × 9
#>       Country  code  Year `Year Code` top10 bot10  gini b40_cons
#>          <chr> <chr> <int>       <chr> <dbl> <dbl> <dbl>    <dbl>
#> 1 Afghanistan   AFG  1974      YR1974    NA    NA    NA       NA
#> 2 Afghanistan   AFG  1975      YR1975    NA    NA    NA       NA
#> 3 Afghanistan   AFG  1976      YR1976    NA    NA    NA       NA
#> 4 Afghanistan   AFG  1977      YR1977    NA    NA    NA       NA
#> # ... with 6,921 more rows, and 1 more variables: gdp_percap <dbl>
```

followed by:

```
wb_ineq %>%
  select(Year, gini)
#> # A tibble: 6,925 × 2
#>     Year   gini
#>    <int> <dbl>
#> 1  1974    NA
#> 2  1975    NA
#> 3  1976    NA
#> 4  1977    NA
#> # ... with 6,921 more rows
```

Explain in your own words what changes each time.

2. Use chained **dplyr** functions to answer the following question: in which year did countries without an *a* in their name have the lowest level of inequality?

Data Aggregation

Data aggregation involves creating summaries of data based on a grouping variable, in a process that has been referred to as *split-apply-combine*. The end result usually has the same number of rows as there are groups. Because aggregation is a way of condensing datasets, it can be a very useful technique for making sense of large datasets. The following code finds the number of unique countries (country being the grouping variable) from the ghg_ems dataset stored in the **efficient** package:

```
# Package available from github.com/csgillespie/efficient
data(ghg_ems, package = "efficient")
names(ghg_ems)
#> [1] "Country"        "Year"          "Electricity"   "Manufacturing"
#> [5] "Transportation" "Other"         "Fugitive"
nrow(ghg_ems)
#> [1] 7896
```

```
length(unique(ghg_ems$Country))
#> [1] 188
```

Note that while there are almost 8,000 rows, there are fewer than 200 countries. Thus factors would have been a more space-efficient way of storing the country data.

To aggregate the dataset using **dplyr**, you divide the task in to two parts: *group* the dataset first and then summarize, as illustrated next.[3]

```
library("dplyr")
group_by(ghg_ems, Country) %>%
  summarize(mean_eco2 = mean(Electricity, na.rm  = TRUE))
#> # A tibble: 188 × 2
#>       Country mean_eco2
#>         <chr>     <dbl>
#> 1 Afghanistan       NaN
#> 2     Albania     0.641
#> 3     Algeria    23.015
#> 4      Angola     0.791
#> # ... with 184 more rows
```

 The previous example relates to wider programming: how much work should one function do? The work could have been done with a single aggregate() call. However, the Unix philosophy (*http://bit.ly/basicsofunix*) states that programs should "do one thing well," which is how **dplyr**'s functions were designed. Shorter functions are easier to understand and debug. But having too many functions can also make your call stack confusing.

To reinforce the point, this operation is also performed in the following code on the wb_ineq dataset:

```
data(wb_ineq, package = "efficient")
countries = group_by(wb_ineq, Country)
summarize(countries, gini = mean(gini, na.rm  = TRUE))
#> # A tibble: 176 × 2
#>       Country  gini
#>         <chr> <dbl>
#> 1 Afghanistan   NaN
#> 2     Albania  30.4
#> 3     Algeria  37.8
#> 4      Angola  50.6
#> # ... with 172 more rows
```

Note that summarize is highly versatile, and can be used to return a customized range of summary statistics:

---

3 The equivalent code in base R is e_ems = aggregate(ghg_ems$Electricity, list(ghg_ems$Country), mean, na.rm = TRUE, data = ghg_ems); nrow(ghg_ems).

```
summarize(countries,
  # number of rows per country
  obs = n(),
  med_t10 = median(top10, na.rm  = TRUE),
  # standard deviation
  sdev = sd(gini, na.rm  = TRUE),
  # number with gini > 30
  n30 = sum(gini > 30, na.rm  = TRUE),
  sdn30 = sd(gini[ gini > 30 ], na.rm  = TRUE),
  # range
  dif = max(gini, na.rm  = TRUE) - min(gini, na.rm  = TRUE)
  )
#> # A tibble: 176 × 7
#>       Country  obs med_t10  sdev   n30  sdn30    dif
#>         <chr> <int>   <dbl> <dbl> <int>  <dbl> <dbl>
#> 1 Afghanistan    40      NA   NaN     0     NA     NA
#> 2     Albania    40    24.4  1.25     3  0.364   2.78
#> 3     Algeria    40    29.8  3.44     2  3.437   4.86
#> 4      Angola    40    38.6 11.30     2 11.300  15.98
#> # ... with 172 more rows
```

To showcase the power of summarize() used on a grouped_df, the previous code reports a wide range of customized summary statistics *per country*:

- The number of rows in each country group
- Standard deviation of Gini indices
- Median proportion of income earned by the top 10%
- The number of years in which the Gini index was greater than 30
- The standard deviation of Gini index values over 30
- The range of Gini index values reported for each country

Exercises

1. Refer back to the greenhouse gas emissions example at the outset of section "Efficient Data Processing with dplyr" on page 108, in which we found the top three countries in terms of emissions growth in the transport sector.

   a. Explain in words what is going on in each line.

   b. Try to find the top three countries in terms of emissions in 2012—how is the list different?

2. Explore **dplyr**'s documentation, starting with the introductory vignette, accessed by entering vignette("introduction") (*https://cran.rstudio.com/web/packages/dplyr/vignettes/introduction.html*).

3. Test additional **dplyr** *verbs* on the wb_ineq dataset. (More vignette names can be discovered by typing `vignette(package = "dplyr")`.)

Nonstandard Evaluation

The final thing to say about **dplyr** does not relate to the data but to the syntax of the functions. Note that many of the arguments in the code examples in this section are provided as raw names; they are raw variable names not surrounded by quotation marks (e.g., `Country` rather than `"Country"`). This is called nonstandard evaluation (NSE) (see `vignette("nse")`). NSE was used deliberately, with the aim of making the functions more efficient for interactive use. NSE reduces typing and allows autocompletion in RStudio.

This is fine when using R interactively. But when you'd like to use R noninteractively, code is generally more robust using standard evaluation because it minimizes the chance of creating obscure scope-related bugs. Using standing evaluation also avoids having to declare global variables if you include the code in a package. For this reason, most functions in **tidyr** and **dplyr** have two versions: one that uses NSE (the default) and another that uses standard evaluation and requires the variable names to be provided in quotation marks. The standard evaluation versions of functions are denoted with the affix _. This is illustrated in the following code with the `gather()` function, used previously:

```
# 1: Default NSE function
group_by(cars, cut(speed, c(0, 10, 100))) %>% summarize(mean(dist))
#> # A tibble: 2 × 2
#>   `cut(speed, c(0, 10, 100))` `mean(dist)`
#>                        <fctr>        <dbl>
#> 1                      (0,10]         15.8
#> 2                    (10,100]         49.0
# 2: Standard evaluation using quote marks
group_by_(cars, "cut(speed, c(0, 10, 100))") %>% summarize_("mean(dist)")
#> # A tibble: 2 × 2
#>   `cut(speed, c(0, 10, 100))` `mean(dist)`
#>                        <fctr>        <dbl>
#> 1                      (0,10]         15.8
#> 2                    (10,100]         49.0
# 3: Standard evaluation using formula, tilde notation
# (recommended standard evaluation method)
group_by_(cars, ~cut(speed, c(0, 10, 100))) %>% summarize_(~mean(dist))
#> # A tibble: 2 × 2
#>   `cut(speed, c(0, 10, 100))` `mean(dist)`
#>                        <fctr>        <dbl>
#> 1                      (0,10]         15.8
#> 2                    (10,100]         49.0
```

Combining Datasets

The usefulness of a dataset can sometimes be greatly enhanced by combining it with other data. If we could merge the global ghg_ems dataset with geographic data, for example, we could visualize the spatial distribution of climate pollution. For the purposes of this section, we join ghg_ems to the world data provided by **ggmap** to illustrate the concepts and methods of data *joining* (also referred to as *merging*).

```
library("ggmap")
world = map_data("world")
names(world)
#> [1] "long"       "lat"        "group"      "order"      "region"     "subregion"
```

Visually compare this new dataset of the world with ghg_ems (e.g., via View(world); View(ghg_ems)). It is clear that the column region in the former contains the same information as Country in the latter. This will be the *joining variable*; renaming it in world will make the join more efficient.

```
world = rename(world, Country = region)
ghg_ems$All = rowSums(ghg_ems[3:7])
```

 Ensure that both joining variables have the same class (combining character and factor columns can cause havoc).

How large is the overlap between ghg_ems$Country and world$Country? We can find out using the %in% operator, which finds out how many elements in one vector match those in another vector. Specifically, we will find out how many *unique* country names from ghg_ems are present in the world dataset:

```
unique_countries_ghg_ems = unique(ghg_ems$Country)
unique_countries_world = unique(world$Country)
matched = unique_countries_ghg_ems %in% unique_countries_world
table(matched)
#> matched
#> FALSE  TRUE
#>    20   168
```

This comparison exercise has been fruitful: most of the countries in the co2 dataset exist in the world dataset. But what about the 20 country names that do not match? We can identify these as follows:

```
(unmatched_countries_ghg_ems = unique_countries_ghg_ems[!matched])
#>  [1] "Antigua & Barbuda"     "Bahamas, The"
#>  [3] "Bosnia & Herzegovina"  "Congo, Dem. Rep."
#>  [5] "Congo, Rep."           "Cote d'Ivoire"
#>  [7] "European Union (15)"   "European Union (28)"
```

```
#>  [9] "Gambia, The"                "Korea, Dem. Rep. (North)"
#> [11] "Korea, Rep. (South)"         "Macedonia, FYR"
#> [13] "Russian Federation"          "Saint Kitts & Nevis"
#> [15] "Saint Vincent & Grenadines"  "Sao Tome & Principe"
#> [17] "Trinidad & Tobago"           "United Kingdom"
#> [19] "United States"               "World"
```

It is clear from the output that some of the nonmatches (e.g., the European Union) are not countries at all. However, others such as Gambia and the United States clearly should have matches. *Fuzzy matching* can help find which countries *do* match, as illustrated by the first nonmatching country here:

```
(unmatched_country = unmatched_countries_ghg_ems[1])
#> [1] "Antigua & Barbuda"
unmatched_world_selection = agrep(pattern = unmatched_country,
    unique_countries_world, max.distance = 10)
unmatched_world_countries = unique_countries_world[unmatched_world_selection]
```

What just happened? We verified that the first unmatching country in the ghg_ems dataset was not in the world country names. So we used the more powerful agrep to search for fuzzy matches (with the max.distance argument set to 10). The results show that the country Antigua & Barbuda from the ghg_ems data matches *two* countries in the world dataset. We can update the names in the dataset we are joining to accordingly:

```
world$Country[world$Country %in% unmatched_world_countries] =
    unmatched_countries_ghg_ems[1]
```

This code reduces the number of country names in the world dataset by replacing *both* "Antigua" and "Barbuda" with "Antigua & Barbuda". This would not work the other way around: how would one know whether to change "Antigua & Barbuda" to "Antigua" or to "Barbuda"?

Thus fuzzy matching is still a laborious process that must be complemented by human judgment. It takes a human to know for sure that United States is represented as USA in the world dataset, without risking false matches via agrep.

Working with Databases

Instead of loading all the data into RAM, as R does, databases query data from the hard disk. This can allow a subset of a very large dataset to be defined and read into R quickly, without having to load it first. R can connect to databases in a number of ways, which are briefly touched on below. The subject of databases is a large area undergoing rapid evolution. Rather than aiming at comprehensive coverage, we will provide pointers to developments that enable efficient access to a wide range of database types. An up-to-date history of R's interfaces to databases can be found in the README of the **DBI** package (*http://bit.ly/DBIREADME*), which provides a common interface and set of classes for driver packages (such as **RSQLite**).

RODBC is a veteran package for querying external databases from within R, using the Open Database Connectivity (ODBC) API. The functionality of **RODBC** is described in the package's vignette (see `vignette("RODBC")`), and today its main use is to provide an R interface to SQL Server databases, which lack a **DBI** interface.

The **DBI** package is a unified framework for accessing databases that allows for other drivers to be added as modular packages. Thus new packages that build on **DBI** can be seen partly as a replacements of **RODBC** (**RMySQL**, **RPostgreSQL**, and **RSQLite**) (see `vignette("backend")` for more on how **DBI** drivers work). Because the **DBI** syntax applies to a wide range of database types, we use it here with a worked example.

Imagine you have access to a database that contains the ghg_ems dataset.

```
# Connect to a database driver
library("RSQLite")
con = dbConnect(SQLite(), dbname = ghg_db) # Also username & password arguments
dbListTables(con)
rs = dbSendQuery(con, "SELECT * FROM `ghg_ems` WHERE (`Country` != 'World')")
df_head = dbFetch(rs, n = 6) # extract first 6 row
```

The preceding code chunk shows how the function `dbConnect` connects to an external database—in this case, a MySQL database. The `username` and `password` arguments are used to establish the connection. Next, we query which tables are available with `dbListTables`, query the database (without yet extracting the results to R) with `dbSendQuery`, and, finally, load the results into R with `dbFetch`.

> Be sure never to release your password by entering it directly into the command. Instead, we recommend saving sensitive information such as database passwords and API keys in *.Renviron*, described in Chapter 2. Assuming you had saved your password as the environment variable PSWRD, you could enter `pwd = Sys.getenv("PSWRD")` to minimize the risk of exposing your password through accidentally releasing the code or your session history.

Recently there has been a shift to the *noSQL* approach to storing large datasets. This is illustrated by the emergence and uptake of software such as MongoDB and Apache Cassandra that have R interfaces via packages **mongolite** (*http://bit.ly/mongoliteR*) and **RJDBC** (*http://bit.ly/RJDBCpackage*), which can connect to Apache Cassandra data stores and any source compliant with the Java Database Connectivity (JDBC) API.

MonetDB is a recent alternative to relational and noSQL approaches that offers substantial efficiency advantages for handling large datasets (Kersten et al. 2011). A tutorial on the MonetDB website (*http://bit.ly/monetDBR*) provides an excellent introduction to handling databases from within R.

There are many wider considerations in relation to databases that we will not cover here: who will manage and maintain the database? How will it be backed up locally (local copies should be stored to reduce reliance on the network)? What is the appropriate database for your project? These issues can have major effects on efficiency, especially on large, data-intensive projects. However, we will not cover them here because it is a fast-moving field. Instead, we direct the interested reader toward resources on the subject, including:

- The website for **sparklyr** (*http://spark.rstudio.com/*), a recently created package for efficiently interfacing with the Apache Spark stack.
- db-engines.com/en/, a website comparing the relative merits of different databases.
- The databases vignette from the **dplyr** package.
- Getting started with MongoDB in R (*http://bit.ly/MongoDBR*), an introductory vignette on nonrelational databases and map reduce from the **mongolite** package.

Databases and dplyr

To access a database in R via **dplyr**, you must use one of the src_*() functions to create a source. Continuing with the SQLite example previously given, you would create a tbl object that can be queried by **dplyr** as follows:

```
library("dplyr")
ghg_db = src_sqlite(ghg_db)
ghg_tbl = tbl(ghg_db, "ghg_ems")
```

The ghg_tbl object can then be queried in a similar way as a standard data frame. For example, suppose we wished to filter by Country. Then we use the filter() function as before:

```
rm_world = ghg_tbl %>%
    filter(Country != "World")
```

In this code, **dplyr** has actually generated the necessary SQL command, which can be examined using explain(rm_world). When working with databases, **dplyr** uses lazy evaluation: the data is only fetched at the last moment when it's needed. The SQL command associated with rm_world hasn't yet been executed; this is why tail(rm_world) doesn't work. By using lazy evaluation, **dplyr** is more efficient at handling large data structures because it avoids unnecessary copying. When you want your SQL command to be executed, use collect(rm_world).

The final stage when working with databases in R is to disconnect:

```
dbDisconnect(conn = con)
```

Exercises

Follow the worked example here to create and query a database on land prices in the UK using **dplyr** as a frontend to an SQLite database. The first stage is to read in the data:

```
# See help("land_df", package="efficient") for details
data(land_df, package = "efficient")
```

The next stage is to create an SQLite database to hold the data:

```
# install.packages("RSQLite") # Requires RSQLite package
my_db = src_sqlite("land.sqlite3", create = TRUE)
land_sqlite = copy_to(my_db, land_df, indexes = list("postcode", "price"))
```

1. What class is the new object land_sqlite?

2. Why did we use the indexes argument?

   From the preceding code, we can see that we have created a tbl. This can be accessed using **dplyr** in the same way as any data frame can. Now we can query the data. You can use SQL code to query the database directly or use standard **dplyr** verbs on the table.

   ```
   # Method 1: using sql
   tbl(my_db, sql('SELECT "price", "postcode", "old/new"  FROM land_df'))
   #> Source:   query [?? x 3]
   #> Database: sqlite 3.8.6 [land.sqlite3]
   #>
   #>    price postcode `old/new`
   #>    <int>    <chr>     <chr>
   #> 1  84000  CW9 5EU         N
   #> 2 123500 TR13 8JH         N
   #> 3 217950 PL33 9DL         N
   #> 4 147000 EX39 5XT         N
   #> # ... with more rows
   ```

3. How would you perform the same query using select()? Try it to see if you get the same result (hint: use backticks for the old/new variable name).

   ```
   #> Source:   query [?? x 3]
   #> Database: sqlite 3.8.6 [land.sqlite3]
   #>
   #>    price postcode `old/new`
   #>    <int>    <chr>     <chr>
   #> 1  84000  CW9 5EU         N
   #> 2 123500 TR13 8JH         N
   #> 3 217950 PL33 9DL         N
   ```

```
#> 4 147000 EX39 5XT        N
#> # ... with more rows
```

Data Processing with data.table

data.table is a mature package for fast data processing that presents an alternative to **dplyr**. There is some controversy about which is more appropriate for different tasks.[4] Which is more efficient to some extent depends on personal preferences and what you are used to. Both are powerful and efficient packages that take time to learn, so it is best to learn one and stick with it, rather than have the duality of using two for similar purposes. There are situations in which one works better than another: **dplyr** provides a more consistent and flexible interface (e.g., with its interface to databases, demonstrated in the previous section), so for most purposes we recommend learning **dplyr** first if you are new to both packages. **dplyr** can also be used to work with the data.table class used by the **data.table** package so you can get the best of both worlds.

data.table is faster than **dplyr** for some operations and offers some functionality unavailable in other packages, however, and has a mature and advanced user community. **data.table** supports rolling joins (*http://bit.ly/datatablerollingjoins*), which allow rows in one table to be selected based on proximity between shared variables (typically time) and non-equi joins (*http://bit.ly/non-equijoins*) where join criteria can be inequalities rather than equal to.

This section provides a few examples to illustrate how **data.table** is unique and (at the risk of inflaming the debate further) some benchmarks you can use to explore which is more efficient. As emphasized throughout the book, efficient code writing is often more important than efficient execution on many everyday tasks, so to some extent it's a matter of preference.

The foundational object class of **data.table** is the data.table. Like **dplyr**'s tbl_df, **data.table**'s data.table objects behave in the same way as the base data.frame class. However, the **data.table** paradigm has some unique features that make it highly computationally efficient for many common tasks in data analysis. Building on subsetting methods using [and filter(), mentioned previously, we'll see **data.tables**'s unique approach to subsetting. Like base R, **data.table** uses square brackets but (unlike base R but like **dplyr**) uses nonstandard evaluation, so you need not refer to the object name inside the brackets:

---

4 One question (*http://bit.ly/datatablevsdplyr*) on the Stack Overflow website titled "data.table vs dplyr" illustrates this controversy and delves into the philosophy underlying each approach.

```
library("data.table")
data(wb_ineq_renamed) # from the efficient package
wb_ineq_dt = data.table(wb_ineq_renamed) # convert to data.table class
aus3a = wb_ineq_dt[Country == "Australia"]
```

 Note that the square brackets do not need a comma to refer to rows with data.table objects; in base R, you would write wb_ineq_renamed[wb_ineq_renamed$Country == "Australia",].

To boost performance, you can set *keys*, analogous to *primary keys in databases*. These are *supercharged rownames* (*http://bit.ly/keysfastbinary*) that order the table based on one or more variables. This allows a *binary search* algorithm to subset the rows of interest, which is much, much faster than the *vector scan* approach used in base R (see `vignette("datatable-keys-fast-subset")`). **data.table** uses the key values for subsetting by default so the variable does not need to be mentioned again. Instead, using keys, the search criteria is provided as a list (invoked in the following code chunk with the concise .() syntax, which is synonymous with `list()`).

```
setkey(wb_ineq_dt, Country)
aus3b = wb_ineq_dt[.("Australia")]
```

The result is the same, so why add the extra stage of setting the key? The reason is that this one-off sorting operation can lead to substantial performance gains in situations where repeatedly subsetting rows on large datasets consumes a large proportion of computational time in your workflow. This is illustrated in Figure 6-1, which compares four methods of subsetting incrementally larger versions of the wb_ineq dataset.

Figure 6-1 demonstrates that **data.table** is *much faster* than base R and **dplyr** at subsetting. As with using external packages used to read in data (see "Plain-Text Formats" on page 88), the relative benefits of **data.table** improve with dataset size, approaching a ~70-fold improvement on base R and a ~50-fold improvement on **dplyr** as the dataset size reaches half a gigabyte. Interestingly, even the *nonkey* implementation of the **data.table** subset method is faster than the alternatives. This is because **data.table** creates a key internally by default before subsetting. The process of creating the key accounts for the ~10 fold speed-up in cases where the key has been pregenerated.

This section has introduced **data.table** as a complimentary approach to base and **dplyr** methods for data processing. It offers performance gains due to its implementation in C and the use of *keys* for subsetting tables. **data.table** offers much more, however, including: highly efficient data reshaping, dataset merging (also known as joining, as with `left_join()` in **dplyr**), and grouping. For further information on **data.table**, we recommend reading the package's `datatable-intro` (*http://bit.ly/data*

tableintro), `datatable-reshape` (*http://bit.ly/datatablereshape*), and `datatable-reference-semantics` (*http://bit.ly/datatablerefsem*) vignettes.

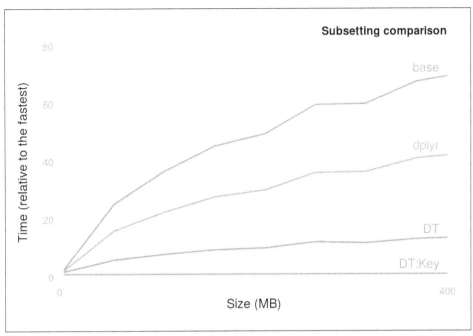

Figure 6-1. Benchmark illustrating the performance gains to be expected for different dataset sizes

References

Wickham, Hadley. 2014b. "Tidy Data." *The Journal of Statistical Software* 14 (5).

Codd, E. F. 1979. "Extending the database relational model to capture more meaning." *ACM Transactions on Database Systems* 4 (4): 397–434. doi:10.1145/320107.320109 (*http://bit.ly/extenddbmodel*).

Spector, Phil. 2008. *Data Manipulation with R*. Springer Science & Business Media.

Sanchez, Gaston. 2013. "Handling and Processing Strings in R." *Trowchez Editions.* http://bit.ly/handlingstringsR.

Grolemund, G., and H. Wickham. 2016. *R for Data Science*. O'Reilly Media.

Wickham, Hadley. 2010. "Stringr: Modern, Consistent String Processing." *The R Journal* 2 (2): 38–40.

Kersten, Martin L, Stratos Idreos, Stefan Manegold, Erietta Liarou, and others. 2011. "The Researcher's Guide to the Data Deluge: Querying a Scientific Database in Just a Few Seconds." *PVLDB Challenges and Visions* 3.

## CHAPTER 7

Efficient Optimization

Donald Knuth (*https://en.wikiquote.org/wiki/Donald_Knuth*) is a legendary American computer scientist who developed a number of the key algorithms that we use today (see, for example, ?Random). On the subject of optimization, he gave this advice:

> The real problem is that programmers have spent far too much time worrying about efficiency in the wrong places and at the wrong times; premature optimization is the root of all evil (or at least most of it) in programming.

Knuth's point is that it is easy to undertake code optimization inefficiently. When developing code, the causes of inefficiencies may shift so that what originally caused slowness at the beginning of your work may not be relevant at a later stage. This means that time spent optimizing code early in the developmental stage could be wasted. Even worse, there is a trade-off between code speed and code readability; we've already made this trade-off once by using readable (but slow) R compared with verbose C code!

For this reason, this chapter is part of the latter half of the book. The previous chapters deliberately focused on concepts, packages, and functions to increase efficiency. These are (relatively) easy ways of saving time that, once implemented, will work for future projects. Code optimization, by contrast, is an advanced topic that should only be tackled once low hanging fruit for efficiency gains have been taken.

In this chapter we assume that you already have well-developed code that is mature conceptually and has been tried and tested. Now you want to optimize this code, but not prematurely. The chapter is organized as follows. First, we begin with general hints and tips about optimizing base R code. Code profiling can identify key bottlenecks in the code in need of optimization, and this is covered in the next section. "Parallel Computing" on page 139 discusses how parallel code can overcome efficiency bottlenecks for some problems. The final section explains how Rcpp can be used to efficiently incorporate C++ code into an R analysis.

Prerequisites

In this chapter, some of the examples require a working C++ compiler. The installation method depends on your operating system:

Linux

A compiler should already be installed. Otherwise, install r-base and a compiler will be installed as a dependency.

Mac

Install Xcode.

Windows

Install Rtools (*http://cran.r-project.org/bin/windows/*). Make sure you select the version that corresponds to your version of R.

The packages used in this chapter are:

```
library("microbenchmark")
library("ggplot2movies")
library("profvis")
library("Rcpp")
```

Top Five Tips for Efficient Optimization

1. Before you start to optimize you code, ensure that you know where the bottleneck lies; use a code profiler.

2. If the data in your data frame is all of the same type, consider converting it to a matrix for a speed boost.

3. Use specialized row and column functions whenever possible.

4. The **parallel** package is ideal for Monte Carlo simulations.

5. For optimal performance, consider rewriting key parts of your code in C++.

Code Profiling

Often you will have working code, but simply want it to run faster. In some cases, it's obvious where the bottleneck lies. Sometimes you will guess, relying on intuition. A drawback of this is that you could be wrong and waste time optimizing the wrong piece of code. To make slow code run faster, it is important to first determine where the slow code lives. This is the purpose of code profiling.

The Rprof() function is a built-in tool for profiling the execution of R expressions. At regular time intervals, the profiler stops the R interpreter, records the current function call stack, and saves the information to a file. The results from Rprof() are stochastic. Each time we run a function R, the conditions have changed. Hence, each time you profile your code, the result will be slightly different.

Unfortunately, Rprof() is not user-friendly. For this reason, we recommend using the **profvis** package for profiling your R code. **profvis** provides an interactive graphical interface for visualizing code-profiling data from Rprof().

Getting Started with profvis

After installing **profvis** (e.g., with install.packages("profvis")), it can be used to profile R code. As a simple example, we will use the movies dataset, which contains information on about 60,000 movies. First, we'll select movies that are classed as comedies, then plot the year the movie was made verus the movie rating and draw a local polynomial regression line to pick out the trend. The main function from the **profvis** package is profvis(), which profiles the code and creates an interactive HTML page of the results. The first argument of profvis() is the R expression of interest. This can be many lines long:

```
library("profvis")
profvis({
  data(movies, package = "ggplot2movies") # Load data
  movies = movies[movies$Comedy == 1,]
  plot(movies$year, movies$rating)
  model = loess(rating ~ year, data = movies) # loess regression line
  j = order(movies$year)
  lines(movies$year[j], model$fitted[j]) # Add line to the plot
})
```

The previous code provides an interactive HTML page (the Figure 7-1). On the left side is the code and on the right is a flame graph (the horizontal direction is time in milliseconds and the vertical direction is the call stack).

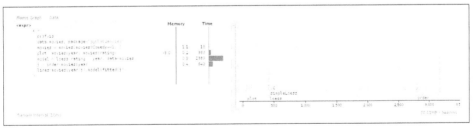

Figure 7-1. Output from profvis

The left-hand panel gives the amount of time spent on each line of code. It shows that the majority of time is spent calculating the loess() smoothing line. The bottom line of the right panel also highlights that most of the execution time is spent on the

loess() function. Traveling up the function, we see that loess() calls simpleLo
ess(), which in turn calls the .C() function.

The conclusion from this graph is that if optimization were required, it would make
sense to focus on the loess() and possibly the order() function calls.

Example: Monopoly Simulation

Monopoly is a board game that originated in the United States over 100 years ago.
The objective of the game is to go around the board and purchase squares (properties). If other players land on your properties, they have to pay a tax. The player with
the most money at the end of the game wins. To make things more interesting, there
are Chance and Community Chest squares. If you land on one of these squares, you
draw a card, which may send you to other parts of the board. The other special square
is Jail. One way of entering Jail is to roll three successive doubles.

The **efficient** package contains a Monte Carlo function for simulating a simplified
game of monopoly. By keeping track of where a person lands when going around the
board, we obtain an estimate of the probability of landing on a certain square. The
entire code is around 100 lines long. In order for **profvis** to fully profile the code, the
efficient package needs to be installed from source:

```
devtools::install_github("csgillespie/efficient", args = "--with-keep.source")
```

The function can then be profiled via the following code, which results in Figure 7-2.

```
library("efficient")
profvis(simulate_monopoly(10000))
```

Figure 7-2. Code profiling for simulating the game of Monopoly

The output from **profvis** shows that the vast majority of time (around 65%) is spent in the move_square() function.

In Monopoly, moving around the board is complicated by the fact that rolling a double (a pair of 1s, 2s, ..., 6s) is special:

- Roll two dice (total1): total_score = total1.
- If you get a double, roll again (total2) and total_score = total1 + total2.
- If you get a double, roll again (total3) and total_score = total1 + total2 + total3.
- If roll three is a double, go to Jail; otherwise, move total_score.

The function move_square() captures this logic. Now that we know where the code is slow, how can we speed up the computation? In the next section, we will discuss standard techniques that can be used. We will then revisit this example.

Efficient Base R

In R, there is often more than one way to solve a problem. In this section, we highlight standard tricks or alternative methods that may improve performance.

The if() Versus ifelse() Functions

ifelse() is a vectorized version of the standard control-flow function if(test) if_yes else if_no that works as follows:

```
ifelse(test, if_yes, if_no)
```

In the preceding imaginary example, the return value is filled with elements from the if_yes and if_no arguments that are determined by whether the element of test is TRUE or FALSE. For example, suppose we have a vector of exam marks. ifelse() could be used to classify them as pass or fail:

```
marks = c(25, 55, 75)
ifelse(marks >= 40, "pass", "fail")
#> [1] "fail" "pass" "pass"
```

If the length of the test condition is equal to 1 (i.e., length(test) == 1), then the standard conditional statement

```
mark = 25
if(mark >= 40) {
  "pass"
} else {
  "fail"
}
```

is around five to ten times faster than `ifelse(mark >= 40, "pass", "fail")`.

An additional quirk of `ifelse()` is that although it is more *programmer efficient*, as it is more concise and understandable than multiline alternatives, it is often less *computationally efficient* than a more verbose alternative. This is illustrated with the following benchmark, in which the second option runs about 20 times faster, despite the results being identical:

```
marks = runif(n = 10e6, min = 30, max = 99)
system.time({
  result1 = ifelse(marks >= 40, "pass", "fail")
})
#>    user  system elapsed
#>   4.293   0.351   4.667
system.time({
  result2 = rep("fail", length(marks))
  result2[marks >= 40] = "pass"
})
#>    user  system elapsed
#>   0.192   0.052   0.244
identical(result1, result2)
#> [1] TRUE
```

There is talk on the R-devel email (*http://bit.ly/ifelsespeed*) list of speeding up `ifelse()` in base R. A simple solution is to use the `if_else()` function from **dplyr**, although, as discussed in the same thread, it cannot replace `ifelse()` in all situations. For our exam result test example, `if_else()` works fine and is much faster than base R's implementation (although it is still around three times slower than the hardcoded solution):

```
system.time({
  result3 = dplyr::if_else(marks >= 40, "pass", "fail")
})
#>    user  system elapsed
#>   1.065   0.188   1.253
identical(result1, result3)
#> [1] TRUE
```

Sorting and Ordering

Sorting a vector is relatively quick; sorting a vector of length 10^7 takes around 0.01 seconds. If you only sort a vector once at the top of a script, then don't worry too much about this. However, if you are sorting inside a loop or in a Shiny application, then it can be worthwhile thinking about how to optimize this operation.

There are currently three sorting algorithms, `c("shell", "quick", "radix")`, that can be specified in the `sort()` function, with `radix` being a new addition to R 3.3. Typically, the `radix` (the nondefault option) is the most computationally efficient option for most situations (it is around 20% faster when sorting a large vector of doubles).

Another useful trick is to partially order the results. For example, if you only want to display the top 10 results, then use the `partial` argument (i.e., `sort(x, partial = 1:10)`). For very large vectors, this can give a three-fold speed increase.

Reversing Elements

The `rev()` function provides a reversed version of its argument. If you wish to sort in increasing order, `sort(x, decreasing = TRUE)` is marginally (around 10%) faster than `rev(sort(x))`.

Which Indices are TRUE?

To determine which index of a vector or array is `TRUE`, we would typically use the `which()` function. If we want to find the index of just the minimum or maximum value (i.e., `which(x == min(x))`), then using the efficient `which.min()`/`which.max()` variants can be orders of magnitude faster (see Figure 7-3).

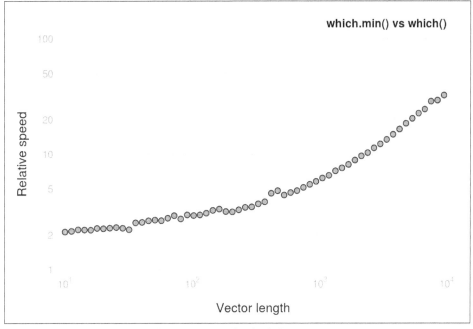

Figure 7-3. Comparison of which.min() with which()

Converting Factors to Numerics

A factor is just a vector of integers with associated levels. Occasionally, we want to convert a factor into its numerical equivalent. The most efficient way of doing this (especially for long factors) is:

```
as.numeric(levels(f))[f]
```

Logical AND and OR

The logical AND (&) and OR (|) operators are vectorized functions and are typically used during multicriteria subsetting operations. The following code, for example, returns TRUE for all elements of x greater than 0.4 or less than 0.6:

```
x < 0.4 | x > 0.6
#> [1]  TRUE FALSE  TRUE
```

When R executes this comparison, it will always calculate x > 0.6 regardless of the value of x < 0.4. In contrast, the nonvectorized version, &&, only executes the second component if needed. This is efficient and leads to neater code:

```
# We only calculate the mean if data doesn't contain NAs
if(!anyNA(x) && mean(x) > 0) {
  # Do something
}
```

compared to

```
if(!anyNA(x)) {
  if(mean(x) > 0) {
    # do something
  }
}
```

However, care must be taken not to use && or || on vectors because it only evaluates the first element of the vector, giving the incorrect answer. This is illustrated here:

```
x < 0.4 || x > 0.6
#> [1] TRUE
```

Row and Column Operations

In data analysis, we often want to apply a function to each column or row of a dataset. For example, we might want to calculate the column or row sums. The apply() function makes this type of operation straightforward.

```
# Second argument: 1 -> rows. 2 -> columns
apply(data_set, 1, function_name)
```

There are optimized functions for calculating row and column sums/means (row Sums(), colSums(), rowMeans(), and colMeans()) that should be used whenever possible. The package **matrixStats** contains many optimized row/column functions.

is.na() and anyNA()

To test whether a vector (or other object) contains missing values, we use the is.na() function. Often we are interested in whether a vector contains *any* missing values. In this case, anyNA(x) is more efficient than any(is.na(x)).

Matrices

A matrix is similar to a data frame: it is a two-dimensional object and subsetting, and other functions work in the same way. However, all matrix elements must have the same type. Matrices tend to be used during statistical calculations. The lm() function, for example, internally converts the data to a matrix before calculating the results; any characters are thus recoded as numeric dummy variables.

Matrices are generally faster than data frames. For example, the datasets ex_mat and ex_df from the **efficient** package each have 1,000 rows and 100 columns and contain the same random numbers. However, selecting rows from the data frame is about 150 times slower than a matrix, as illustrated here:

```
data(ex_mat, ex_df, package = "efficient")
microbenchmark(times = 100, unit = "ms", ex_mat[1, ], ex_df[1, ])
#> Unit: milliseconds
#>        expr     min      lq    mean  median      uq  max neval
#>  ex_mat[1, ] 0.00252 0.00368 0.0565 0.00531 0.00593 5.08   100
#>   ex_df[1, ] 0.77058 0.87406 1.0894 0.96771 1.10045 6.36   100
```

 Use the data.matrix() function to efficiently convert a data frame into a matrix.

The integer data type

Numbers in R are usually stored in double-precision floating-point format (*https://goo.gl/ZA5R8a*), which is described in detail in *A First Course in Statistical Programming with R* (Braun and Murdoch 2007) and "What Every Computer Scientist Should Know About Floating-Point Arithmetic" (Goldberg). The term *double* refers to the fact that on 32-bit systems (for which the format was developed) two memory locations are used to store a single number. Each double-precision number is accurate to about 17 decimal places.

When comparing floating-point numbers, we should be particularly careful because y = sqrt(2) * sqrt(2) is not exactly 2—it's *almost* 2. Using sprintf("%.17f", y) will give you the true value of y (to 17 decimal places).

Integers are another numeric data type. Integers primarily exist to be passed to C or Fortran code. You will not need to create integers for most applications. However, they are occasionally used to optimize subsetting operations. When we subset a data frame or matrix, we are interacting with C code and might be tempted to use integers with the purpose of speeding up our code. For example, if we look at the arguments for the head function

```
args(head.matrix)
#> function (x, n = 6L, ...)
#> NULL
```

Using the : operator automatically creates a vector of integers.

we see that the default argument for n is 6L rather than simply 6 (the L is short for literal and is used to create an integer). This gives a tiny speed boost (around 0.1 microseconds!).

```
x = runif(10)
microbenchmark(head(x, 6.0), head(x, 6L), times = 1000000)
# Unit: microseconds
#         expr   min    lq  mean median    uq    max neval cld
#   head(x, 6) 7.067 8.309 9.058  8.686 9.098 105266 1e+06   a
#  head(x, 6L) 6.947 8.219 8.933  8.594 9.007 106307 1e+06   a
```

Because this function is ubiquitous, this low-level optimization is useful. In general, if you are worried about shaving microseconds off your R code run time, you should probably consider switching to another language.

Integers are more space-efficient. The following code compares the size of an integer vector to that of a standard numeric vector:

```
pryr::object_size(1:10000)
#> 40 kB
pryr::object_size(seq(1, 10000, by = 1.0))
#> 80 kB
```

The results show that the integer version is roughly half the size. However, most mathematical operations will convert the integer vector into a standard numerical vector, as illustrated in the following code chunk:

```
is.integer(1L + 1)
#> [1] FALSE
```

Further storage savings can be obtained using the **bit** package.

Sparse matrices

Another data structure that can be stored efficiently is a sparse matrix. This is simply a matrix where most of the elements are zero. Conversely, if most elements are nonzero, the matrix is considered dense. The proportion of nonzero elements is called the sparsity. Large, sparse matrices often crop up when performing numerical calculations. Typically, our data isn't sparse, but the resulting data structures we create may be sparse. There are a number of techniques/methods used to store sparse matrices. Methods for creating sparse matrices can be found in the **Matrix** package.[1]

As an example, suppose we have a large matrix in which the diagonal elements are nonzero:

```
library("Matrix")
N = 10000
sp = sparseMatrix(1:N, 1:N, x = 1)
m = diag(1, N, N)
```

Both objects contain the same information, but the data is stored differently. Because we have the same value multiple times in the matrix, we only need to store the value once and link it to multiple matrix locations. The matrix object stores each individual element, whereas the sparse matrix object only stores the location of the nonzero elements. This is much more memory-efficient, as illustrated in the following code:

```
pryr::object_size(sp)
#> 161 kB
pryr::object_size(m)
#> 800 MB
```

Exercises

1. Create a vector, x. Benchmark `any(is.na(x))` against `anyNA()`. Do the results vary with the size of the vector?

2. Examine the following function definitions to give you an idea of how integers are used:

   - `tail.matrix()`
   - `lm()`

---

1 Technically this isn't in base R; it's a recommended package.

3. Construct a matrix of integers and a matrix of numerics. Using `pryr::object_size()`, compare the objects.

4. How does the function `seq.int()`, which was used in the `tail.matrix()` function, differ from the standard `seq()` function?

 A related memory-saving idea is to replace `logical` vectors with vectors from the **bit** package, which take up just over 1/30th of the space (but you can't use NAs).

Example: Optimizing the move_square() Function

Figure 7-2 shows that our main bottleneck in simulating the game of Monopoly is the `move_square()` function. Within this function, we spend around 50% of the time creating a data frame, 20% calculating row sums, and the remainder on comparison operations. This piece of code can be optimized fairly easily (while still retaining the same overall structure) by incorporating the following improvements:[2]

- Instead of using `seq(1, 6)` to generate the six possible values of rolling a die, use `1:6`. Also, instead of a data frame, use a matrix and perform a single call to the `sample()` function:

      `matrix(sample(1:6, 6, replace = TRUE), ncol = 2)`

  Overall, this revised line is around 25 times faster; most of the speed boost came from switching to a matrix.

- Use `rowSums()` instead of `apply()`. The `apply()` function call is already faster because we switched from a data frame to a matrix (around three times). Using `rowSums()` with a matrix gives a 10-fold speed boost.

- Use `&&` in the `if` condition; this is about twice as fast as `&`.

Impressively, the refactored code runs 20 times faster than the original code. Compare Figures 7-2 and 7-4 with the main speed boost coming from using a matrix instead of a data frame.

---

2 Solutions are available in the **efficient** package vignette.

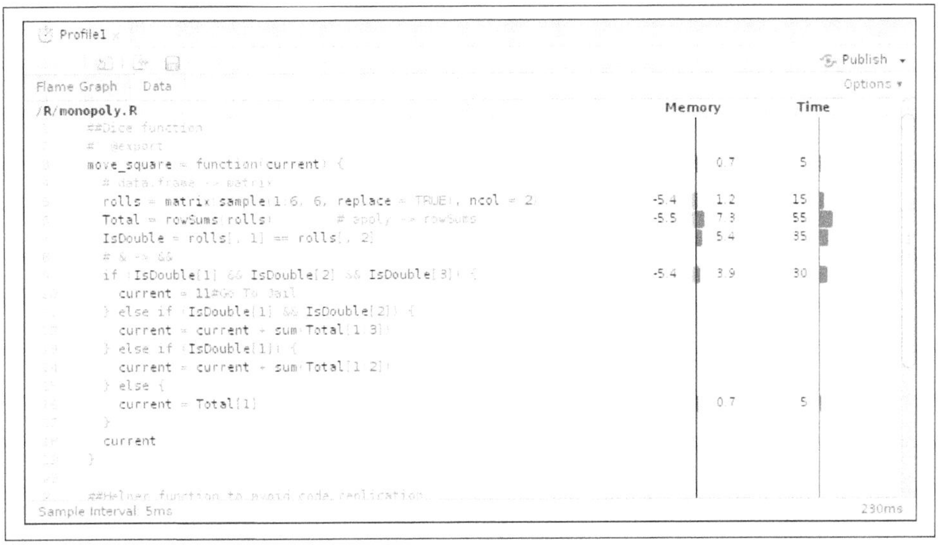

Figure 7-4. Code profiling of the optimized code

Exercise

1. The `move_square()` function shown in Figure 7-4 uses a vectorized solution. Whenever we move, we always roll six dice, then examine the outcome and determine the number of doubles. However, this is potentially wasteful, since the probability of getting one double is 1/6 and two doubles is 1/36. Another method is to only roll additional dice if and when they are needed. Implement and time this solution.

Parallel Computing

This section provides a brief foray into the word of parallel computing. It only looks at methods for parallel computing on *shared memory systems*. This simply means computers in which multiple CPU cores can access the same block (i.e., most laptops and desktops sold worldwide). This section provides a flavor of what is possible; for a fuller account of parallel processing in R, see *Parallel R* by McCallum and Weston (O'Reilly).

The foundational package for parallel computing in R is **parallel**. In recent R versions (since R 2.14.0), this comes preinstalled with base R. The **parallel** package must still be loaded before use, however, and you must manually determine the number of available cores manually as illustrated in the following code:

```
library("parallel")
no_of_cores = detectCores()
```

The value returned by detectCores() turns out to be operating-system and chip-maker dependent; see help("detectCores") for full details. For most standard machines, detectCores() returns the number of simultaneous threads.

Parallel Versions of Apply Functions

The most commonly used parallel applications are parallelized replacements of lapply(), sapply(), and apply(). The parallel implementations and their arguments are shown in the following code example:

```
parLapply(cl, x, FUN, ...)
parApply(cl = NULL, X, MARGIN, FUN, ...)
parSapply(cl = NULL, X, FUN, ..., simplify = TRUE, USE.NAMES = TRUE)
```

The key point is that there is very little difference in arguments between parLapply(), and apply(), so the barrier to using (this form) of parallel computing is low, assuming you are proficient with the apply family of functions. Each of these functions has an argument cl, which is created by a makeCluster() call. This function, among other things, specifies the number of processors to use.

Example: Snakes and Ladders

Parallel computing is ideal for Monte Carlo simulations. Each core independently simulates a realization from the model. At the end, we gather up the results. In the **efficient** package, there is a function that simulates a single game of Snakes and Ladders: snakes_ladders().[3]

The following code illustrates how to simulate N games using sapply():

```
N = 10^4
sapply(1:N, snakes_ladders)
```

Rewriting this code to make use of the **parallel** package is straightforward. Begin by making a cluster object:

```
library("parallel")
cl = makeCluster(4)
```

Then simply swap sapply() for parSapply():

```
parSapply(cl, 1:N, snakes_ladders)
```

---

3 The idea for this example came to one of the authors after a particularly long and dull game of Snakes and Ladders with his son.

It is important to stop the created clusters, as this can lead to memory leaks,[4] as illustrated in the following code:

```
stopCluster(cl)
```

If we achieved perfect parallelization and used a four (or more) core, then we would obtain a four-fold speed up (we set `makeCluster(4)`). However, we rarely get this.

On a multiprocessor computer, this can lead to a four-fold speed-up. However, it is rare to achieve this optimal speed-up since there is always communication between threads.

Exit Functions with Care

Always call `stopCluster()` to free resources when you finish with the cluster object. However, if the parallel code is within a function call that results in an error, the `StopCluster()` command would be omitted.

The `on.exit()` function handles this problem with a minimum of fuss; regardless of how the function ends, `on.exit()` is always called. In the context of parallel programming, we will have something similar to:

```
simulate = function(cores) {
  cl = makeCluster(cores)
  on.exit(stopCluster(cl))
  # Do something
}
```

Another common use of `on.exit()` is with the `par()` function. If you use `par()` to change graphical parameters within a function, `on.exit()` ensures that these parameters are reset to their previous value when the function ends.

Parallel Code under Linux and OS X

If you are using Linux or OS X, then another way of running code in parallel is to use the `mclapply()` and `mcmapply()` functions:

```
# This will run on Windows, but will only use 1 core
mclapply(1:N, snakes_ladders)
```

These functions use forking; that is, creating a new copy of a process running on the CPU. However, Windows does not support this low-level functionality in the way that Linux does. The main advantage of `mclapply()` is that you don't have to start and

---

4 See github.com/npct/pct-shiny/issues/292 (*https://github.com/npct/pct-shiny/issues/292*) for a real-world example of the dangers of not stopping created cores.

stop cluster objects. The big disadvantage is that on Windows machines, you are limited to a single core.

Rcpp

Sometimes R is just slow. You've tried every trick you know, and your code is still crawling along. At this point, you could consider rewriting key parts of your code in another, faster language. R has interfaces to other languages via packages, such as **Rcpp**, **rJava**, **rPython**, and recently **V8**. These provide R interfaces to C++, Java, Python, and JavaScript, respectively. **Rcpp** is the most popular of these (Figure 7-5).

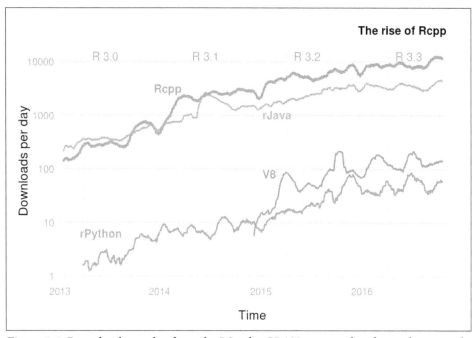

Figure 7-5. Downloads per day from the RStudio CRAN mirror of packages that provide R interfaces to other languages

C++ is a modern, fast, and very well-supported language with libraries for performing many kinds of computational tasks. **Rcpp** makes incorporating C++ code into your R workflow easy.

Although C/Fortran routines can be used using the .Call() function, this is not recommended because using .Call() can be a painful experience. **Rcpp** provides a friendly API that lets you write high-performance code, bypassing R's tricky C API. Typical bottlenecks that C++ addresses are loops and recursive functions.

C++ is a powerful programming language about which entire books have been written. This section therefore is focused on getting started and providing a flavor of what is possible. It is structured as follows. After ensuring that your computer is set up for **Rcpp**, we proceed by = creating a simple C++ function, to show how C++ compares with R ("A Simple C++ Function"). This is converted into an R function using cppFunction() in "The cppFunction() Command" on page 144.

The remainder of the chapter explains C++ data types ("C++ Data Types" on page 145), illustrates how to source C++ code directly ("The sourceCpp() Function" on page 145), explains vectors ("Vectors and Loops" on page 146) and **Rcpp** sugar ("C++ with Sugar on Top" on page 149), and finally provides guidance on further resources on the subject ("Rcpp Resources" on page 150).

A Simple C++ Function

To write and compile C++ functions, you need a working C++ compiler (see "Prerequisites" on page 128). The code in this chapter was generated using version 0.12.7 of **Rcpp**.

Rcpp is well documented, as illustrated by the number of vignettes on the package's CRAN (*https://cran.r-project.org/web/packages/Rcpp/*) page. In addition to its popularity, many other packages depend on **Rcpp**, which can be seen by looking at the Reverse Imports section.

To check that you have everything needed for this chapter, run the following piece of code from the course R package:

```
efficient::test_rcpp()
```

A C++ function is similar to an R function: you pass a set of inputs to a function, some code is run, and a single object is returned. However, there are some key differences:

- In the C++ function, each line must be terminated with ;. In R, we use ; only when we have multiple statements on the same line.

- We must declare object types in the C++ version. In particular, we need to declare the types of the function arguments, the return values, and any intermediate objects we create.

- The function must have an explicit return statement. Similar to R, there can be multiple returns, but the function will terminate when it hits its first return statement.

- You do not use assignment when creating a function.

- Object assignment must use the = sign. The <- operator isn't valid.

- One-line comments can be created using //. Multiline comments are created using /*...*/.

Suppose we want to create a function that adds two numbers together. In R, this would be a simple one-line affair:

```
add_r = function(x, y) x + y
```

In C++, it is a bit more long-winded:

```
/* Return type double
 * Two arguments, also doubles
 */
double add_cpp(double x, double y) {
  double value = x + y;
  return value;
}
```

If we were writing a C++ program, we would also need another function called main(). We would then compile the code to obtain an executable. The executable is platform-dependent. The beauty of using **Rcpp** is that it makes it very easy to call C++ functions from R and the user doesn't have to worry about the platform, compilers, or the R/C++ interface.

The cppFunction() Command

If we pass the C++ function created in the previous section as a text string argument to cppFunction()

```
library("Rcpp")
cppFunction('
  double add_cpp(double x, double y) {
    double value = x + y;
    return value;
  }
')
```

Rcpp will magically compile the C++ code and construct a function that bridges the gap between R and C++. After running the code shown previously, we now have access to the add_cpp() function

```
add_cpp
#> function (x, y)
#> .Primitive(".Call")(<pointer: 0x2b9e590670e0>, x, y)
```

and can call the add_cpp() function in the usual way:

```
add_cpp(1, 2)
#> [1] 3
```

We don't have to worry about compilers. Also, if you include this function in a package, users don't have to worry about any of the **Rcpp** magic. It just works.

C++ Data Types

The most basic type of variable is an integer, `int`. An `int` variable can store a value in the range –32768 to +32767. To store floating-point numbers, there are single-precision numbers (`float`) and double-precision numbers (`double`). A `double` takes twice as much memory as a `float` (in general, we should always work with double-precision numbers unless we have a compiling reason to switch to floats). For single characters, we use the `char` data type.

There is also something called an unsigned int, which goes from 0 to 65,535 and a `long int` that ranges from 0 to $2^{31} - 1$.

A pointer object is a variable that points to an area of memory that has been given a name. Pointers are a very powerful—but primitive—facility contained in the C++ language. They can be very efficient because since rather than passing large objects around, we pass a pointer to the memory location; in other words, rather than pass the house, we just give the address. We won't use pointers in this chapter, but mention them for completeness. Table 7-1 gives an overview.

Table 7-1. Overview of key C++ object types

Type	Description
char	A single character
int	An integer
float	A single-precision floating-point number
double	A double-precision floating-point number
void	A valueless quantity

The sourceCpp() Function

The `cppFunction()` is great for getting small examples up and running. But it is better practice to put your C++ code in a separate file (with file extension *.cpp*) and use the function call `sourceCpp("path/to/file.cpp")` to compile them. However, we do need to include a few headers at the top of the file. The first line we add gives us access to the **Rcpp** functions. The file *Rcpp.h* contains a list of function and class definitions supplied by **Rcpp**. This file will be located where **Rcpp** is installed. The `include` line

```
#include <Rcpp.h>
```

causes the compiler to replace that line with the contents of the named source file. This means that we can access the functions defined by **Rcpp**. To access the **Rcpp** functions, we would have to type `Rcpp::function_1`. To avoid typing `Rcpp::`, we use the namespace facility:

```
using namespace Rcpp;
```

Now we can just type `function_1()`; this is the same concept that R uses for managing function name collisions when loading packages. Above each function we want to export/use in R, we add the tag:

```
// [[Rcpp::export]]
```

 Similar to packages and the `library()` function in R, we access additional functions via `#include`. A standard header to include is `#include <math.h>`, which contains standard mathematics functions.

This would give the complete file:

```
#include <Rcpp.h>
using namespace Rcpp;

// [[Rcpp::export]]
double add_cpp(double x, double y) {
  double value = x + y;
  return value;
}
```

There are two main benefits with putting your C++ functions in separate files. First, we have the benefit of syntax highlighting (RStudio has great support for C++ editing). Second, it's easier to make syntax errors when the switching between R and C++ in the same file. To save space, we'll omit the headers for the remainder of the chapter.

Vectors and Loops

Let's now consider a slightly more complicated example. Here we want to write our own function that calculates the mean. This is just an illustrative example: R's version is much better and more robust to scale differences in our data. For comparison, let's create a corresponding R function—this is the same function we used in Chapter 3. The function takes a single vector x as input and returns the mean value, m:

```
mean_r = function(x) {
  m = 0
  n = length(x)
  for(i in 1:n)
    m = m + x[i] / n
  m
}
```

This is a very bad R function; we should just use the base function mean() for real-world applications. However, the purpose of mean_r() is to provide a comparison for the C++ version, which we will write in a similar way.

In this example, we will let **Rcpp** smooth the interface between C++ and R by using the NumericVector data type. This **Rcpp** data type mirrors the R vector object type. Other common classes are IntegerVector, CharacterVector, and LogicalVector.

In the C++ version of the mean function, we specify the argument types: x (Numeric Vector) and the return value (double). The C++ version of the mean() function is a few lines longer. Almost always, the corresponding C++ version will be, possibly much, longer. In general, R optimizes for reduced development time; C++ optimizes for fast execution time. The corresponding C++ function for calculating the mean is:

```
double mean_cpp(NumericVector x) {
  int i;
  int n = x.size();
  double mean = 0;

  for(i=0; i<n; i++) {
    mean = mean + x[i] / n;
  }
  return mean;
}
```

To use the C++ function, we need to source the file (remember to put the necessary headers in):

```
sourceCpp("src/mean_cpp.cpp")
```

Although the C++ version is similar, there are a few crucial differences.

1. We use the .size() method to find the length of x.

2. The for loop has a more complicated syntax.

   ```
   for (variable initialisation; condition; variable update ) {
     // Code to execute
   }
   ```

   In this example, the loop initializes i = 0 and will continue running until i < n is false. The statement i++ increases the value of i by 1; essentially it's just a shortcut for i = i + 1.

3. Similar to i++, C++ provides other operators to modify variables in place. For example, we could rewrite part of the loop as

   ```
   mean += x[i] / n;
   ```

The previous code adds x[i] / n to the value of mean. Other similar operators are -=, *=, /=, and i--.

4. A C++ vector starts at 0, not 1.

To compare the C++ and R functions, we'll generate some normal random numbers:

```
x = rnorm(1e4)
```

Then call the `microbenchmark()` function (the results are plotted in Figure 7-6).

```
# com_mean_r is the compiled version of mean_r
z = microbenchmark(
  mean(x), mean_r(x), com_mean_r(x), mean_cpp(x),
  times = 1000
)
```

In this simple example, the **Rcpp** variant is around 100 times faster than the corresponding pure R version. This sort of speed-up is not uncommon when switching to an **Rcpp** solution. Notice that the **Rcpp** version and standard base function `mean()` run at roughly the same speed; after all, the base R function is written in C. However, `mean()` uses a more sophisticated algorithm when calculating the mean to ensure accuracy.

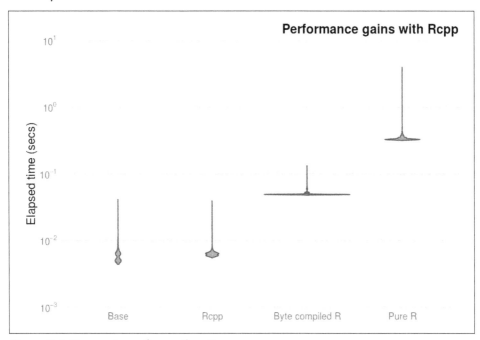

Figure 7-6. Comparison of mean functions

Exercises

Consider the following piece of code:

```
double test1() {
  double a = 1.0 / 81;
  double b = 0;
  for (int i = 0; i < 729; ++ i)
    b = b + a;
  return b;
}
```

1. Save the function `test1()` in a separate file. Make sure it works.

2. Write a similar function in R and compare the speed of the C++ and R versions.

3. Create a function called `test2()`, in which the `double` variables have been replaced by `float`. Do you still get the correct answer?

4. Change `b = b + a` to `b += a` to make your code more like C++.

5. (Difficult!) What's the difference between `i++` and `++i`?

Matrices

Each vector type has a corresponding matrix equivalent: `NumericMatrix`, `IntegerMa trix`, `CharacterMatrix`, and `LogicalMatrix`. We use these types in a similar way to how we used `NumericVectors`. The main differences are:

- When we initialize, we need to specify the number of rows and columns:

```
// 10 rows, 5 columns
NumericMatrix mat(10, 5);
// Length 10
NumericVector v(10);
```

- We subset using ()—i.e., `mat(5, 4)`.

- The first element in a matrix is `mat(0, 0)`—remember that indexes start with 0, not 1.

- To determine the number of rows and columns, we use the `.nrow()` and `.ncol()` methods.

C++ with Sugar on Top

Rcpp sugar brings a higher level of abstraction to C++ code written using the **Rcpp** API. What this means in practice is that we can write C++ code in the style of R. For example, suppose we wanted to find the squared difference of two vectors; a squared residual in regression. In R, we would use

```
sq_diff_r = function(x, y) (x - y)^2
```

Rewriting the function in standard C++ would give

```
NumericVector res_c(NumericVector x, NumericVector y) {
  int i;
  int n = x.size();
  NumericVector residuals(n);
  for(i = 0; i < n; i++) {
    residuals[i] = pow(x[i] - y[i], 2);
  }
  return residuals;
}
```

With **Rcpp** sugar, we can rewrite this code to be more succinct and have more of an R feel:

```
NumericVector res_sugar(NumericVector x, NumericVector y) {
  return pow(x - y, 2);
}
```

In the previous C++ code, the pow() function and x-y are valid due to **Rcpp** sugar. Other functions that are available include the d/q/p/r statistical functions, such as rnorm() and pnorm(). The sweetened versions aren't usually faster than the C++ versions, but typically there's very little difference between the two. However, with the sugared variety, the code is shorter and is constantly being improved.

Exercises

1. Construct an R version (using a for loop rather than the vectorized solution), res_r(), and compare the three function variants.

2. In the previous example, res_sugar() is faster than res_c(). Do you know why?

Rcpp Resources

The aim of this section was to provide an introduction to **Rcpp**. One of the selling points of **Rcpp** is that there is a great deal of documentation available.

- The **Rcpp** website (*http://www.rcpp.org/*).

- The original *Journal of Statistical Software* paper describing **Rcpp** and the follow-up book *Seamless R and C++ Integration with Rcpp* by Eddelbuettel and Francois.

- Hadley Wickham provides a very readable chapter on **Rcpp** in *Advanced R* that goes into a bit more detail than this section.

- The **Rcpp** section on the Stack Overflow (*https://stackoverflow.com/questions/tagged/rcpp*) website. Questions are often answered by the **Rcpp** authors.

References

Braun, John, and Duncan J Murdoch. 2007. *A First Course in Statistical Programming with R*. Vol. 25. Cambridge University Press Cambridge.

Goldberg, David. 1991. "What Every Computer Scientist Should Know About Floating-Point Arithmetic." *ACM Computing Surveys* (CSUR) 23 (1). ACM: 5–48.

McCallum, Ethan, and Stephen Weston. 2011. *Parallel R*. O'Reilly Media.

Eddelbuettel, Dirk, and Romain François. 2011. "Rcpp: Seamless R and C++ Integration." *Journal of Statistical Software* 40 (8): 1–18.

Eddelbuettel, Dirk. 2013. *Seamless R and C++ Integration with Rcpp*. Springer.

Wickham, Hadley. 2014a. *Advanced R*. CRC Press.

## CHAPTER 8

Efficient Hardware

This chapter is odd for a book on R programming. It contains very little code, and yet the chapter has the potential to speed up your algorithms by orders of magnitude. This chapter considers the impact that your computer has on your time.

Your hardware is crucial. It will not only determine how *fast* you can solve your problem, but also whether you can even tackle the problem of interest. This is because everything is loaded in RAM. Of course, having a more powerful computer costs money. The goal is to help you decide whether the benefits of upgrading your hardware are worth that extra cost.

We begin this chapter with a background section on computer storage and memory and how it is measured. Then we consider individual computer components, and conclude with renting machines in the cloud.

Prerequisites

This chapter will focus on assessing your hardware and the benefit of upgrading. We will use the **benchmarkme** package to quantify the effect of changing your CPU.

```
library("benchmarkme")
```

Top Five Tips for Efficient Hardware

1. Use the package **benchmarkme** to assess your CPU's number-crunching ability; is it worth upgrading your hardware?
2. If possible, add more RAM.
3. Double-check that you have installed a 64-bit version of R.
4. Cloud computing is a cost-effective way of obtaining more computer power.

5. Solid-state drives typically won't have much impact on the speed of your R code but will increase your overall productivity because I/0 is much faster.

Background: What Is a Byte?

A computer cannot store "numbers" or "letters." The only thing a computer can store and work with is bits. A bit is binary; it is either a 0 or a 1. In fact, from a physics perspective, a bit is just a blip of electricity that either is or isn't there.

In the past, the ASCII character set dominated computing. This set defines 128 characters including 0 to 9, upper and lowercase alphanumeric, and a few control characters such as a new line. Storing these characters required 7 bits because $2^7 = 128$, but 8 bits were typically used for performance reasons (*http://bit.ly/asciicode8bit*). Table 8-1 gives the binary representation of the first few characters.

Table 8-1. The bit representation of a few ASCII characters

Bit representation	Character
01000001	A
01000010	B
01000011	C
01000100	D
01000101	E
01010010	R

The limitation of only having 256 characters led to the development of Unicode, a standard framework aimed at creating a single character set for every reasonable writing system. Typically, Unicode characters require 16 bits of storage.

Eight bits is one byte, or ASCII character. So two ASCII characters would use two bytes or 16 bits. A pure text document containing 100 characters would use 100 bytes (800 bits). Note that markup, such as font information or metadata, can impose a substantial memory overhead: an empty *.docx* file requires about 3,700 bytes of storage.

When computer scientists first started to think about computer memory, they noticed that $2^{10} = 1024 \simeq 10^3$ and $2^{20} = 1,048,576 \simeq 10^6$, so they adopted the shorthand of kilo- and megabytes. Of course, everyone knew that it was just a short hand, and it was really a binary power. When computers became more widespread, foolish people like you and me just assumed that kilo actually meant 10^3 bytes.

Fortunately, the IEEE Standards Board intervened and created conventional, internationally adopted definitions of the International System of Units (SI) prefixes. So a kilobyte (kB) is $10^3 = 1000$ bytes and a megabyte (MB) is 10^6 bytes or 10^3 kilobytes (see Table 8-2). A petabyte is approximately 100 million drawers filled with text. Astonishingly, Google processes around 20 petabytes of data every day.

Table 8-2. Data-conversion table. Source: http://physics.nist.gov/cuu/Units/binary.html

Factor	Name	Symbol	Origin	Derivation
2^{10}	kibi	Ki	Kilobinary:	$(2^{10})^1$
2^{20}	mebi	Mi	Megabinary:	$(2^{10})^2$
2^{30}	gibi	Gi	Gigabinary:	$(2^{10})^3$
2^{40}	tebi	Ti	Terabinary:	$(2^{10})^4$
2^{50}	pebi	Pi	Petabinary:	$(2^{10})^5$

Even though there is now an agreed upon standard for discussing memory, not everyone follows it. Microsoft Windows, for example, uses 1 MB to mean 2^{20} B. Even more confusing, the capacity of a 1.44 MB floppy disk is a mixture, 1 MB = $10^3 \times 2^{10}$ B. Typically RAM is specified in kibibytes, but hard-drive manufacturers follow the SI standard!

Random Access Memory

Random access memory (RAM) is a type of computer memory that can be accessed randomly: any byte of memory can be accessed without touching the preceding bytes. RAM is found in computers, phones, tablets, and even printers. The amount of RAM R has access to is incredibly important. Since R loads objects into RAM, the amount of RAM you have available can limit the size of dataset you can analyze.

Even if the original dataset is relatively small, your analysis can generate large objects. For example, suppose we want to perform standard cluster analysis. The built-in dataset USAarrests is a data frame with 50 rows and four columns. Each row corresponds to a state in the US:

```
head(USArrests, 3)
#>         Murder Assault UrbanPop Rape
#> Alabama   13.2     236       58 21.2
#> Alaska    10.0     263       48 44.5
#> Arizona    8.1     294       80 31.0
```

If we want to group states that have similar crime statistics, a standard first step is to calculate the distance or similarity matrix:

```
d = dist(USArrests)
```

When we inspect the object size of the original dataset and the distance object using the **pryr** package:

```
pryr::object_size(USArrests)
#> 5.23 kB
```

```
pryr::object_size(d)
#> 14.3 kB
```

We have managed to create an object that is three times larger than the original dataset.

The distance object d is actually a vector that contains the distances in the upper triangular region.

In fact, the object d is a symmetric $n \times n$ matrix, where n is the number of rows in USAarrests. Clearly, as n increases, the size of d increases at a rate of $O(n^2)$. So if our original dataset contained 10,000 records, the associated distance matrix would contain almost 10^8 values. Of course, since the matrix is symmetrical, this corresponds to around 50 million unique values.

A rough rule of thumb is that your RAM should be three times the size of your dataset.

Another benefit of having more onboard RAM is that the *garbage collector*, a process that runs periodically to free up system memory occupied by R, is called less often. It is straightforward to determine how much RAM you have using the **benchmarkme** package:

```
benchmarkme::get_ram()
#> 16.3 GB
```

It is sometimes possible to increase your computer's RAM. On a computer motherboard, there are typically two to four RAM or memory slots. If you have free slots, then you can add more memory. RAM comes in the form of dual in-line memory modules (DIMMs) that can be slotted into the motherboard spaces (see Figure 8-1 for an example).

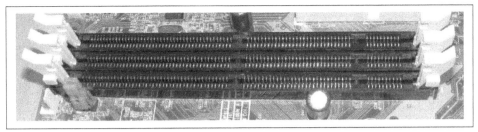

Figure 8-1. Three DIMM slots on a computer motherboard used for increasing the amount of available RAM. Source: Wikimedia (https://www.wikimedia.org/)

However, it is common that all slots are already taken. This means that to upgrade your computer's memory, some or all of the DIMMs will have to be removed. To go from 8 GB to 16 GB, for example, you may have to discard the two 4 GB RAM cards and replace them with two 8 GB cards. Increasing your laptop/desktop from 4 GB to 16 GB or 32 GB is cheap and should definitely be considered. As R Core member Uwe Ligges states:

```
fortunes::fortune(192)
#>
#> RAM is cheap and thinking hurts.
#>      -- Uwe Ligges (about memory requirements in R)
#>         R-help (June 2007)
```

It is a testament to the design of R that it is still relevant and its popularity is growing. Ross Ihaka, one of the originators of the R programming language, made a throwaway comment in 2003:

```
fortunes::fortune(21)
#>
#> I seem to recall that we were targeting 512k Macintoshes. In our dreams
#> we might have seen 16Mb Sun.
#>      -- Ross Ihaka (in reply to the question whether R&R thought when they
#>         started out that they would see R using 16G memory on a dual Opteron
#>         computer)
#>         R-help (November 2003)
```

Considering that a standard smartphone now contains 1 GB of RAM, the fact that R was designed for "basic" computers but can scale across clusters is impressive. R's origins on computers with limited resources helps explain its efficiency at dealing with large datasets.

Exercises

The following two exercises aim to help you determine if it is worthwhile to upgrade your RAM.

1. R loads everything into memory (i.e., your computer's RAM). How much RAM does your computer have?

2. Using your preferred search engine, how much does it cost to double the amount of available RAM on your system?

Hard Drives: HDD Versus SSD

You are using R because you want to analyze data. The data is typically stored on your hard drive, but not all hard drives are equal. Unless you have a fairly expensive laptop, your computer probably has a standard hard disk drive (HDD). HDDs were first introduced by IBM in 1956. Data is stored using magnetism on a rotating platter, as shown in Figure 8-2. The faster the platter spins, the faster the HDD can perform. Many laptop drives spin at either 5,400 or 7,200 RPM (revolutions per minute). The major advantage of HDDs is that they are cheap, making a 1 TB laptop standard.

 In the authors' experience, having an SSD drive doesn't make too much of a difference to R. However, the reduction in boot time and general tasks makes an SSD drive a wonderful purchase.

Figure 8-2. A standard 2.5" hard drive, found in most laptops. Source: Wikimedia (https://en.wikipedia.org/wiki/Hard_disk_drive)

Solid-state drives (SSDs) can be thought of as large but more sophisticated versions of USB sticks. They have no moving parts, and information is stored in microchips. Since there are no moving parts, reading/writing is much quicker. SSDs have other benefits: they are quieter, allow faster boot time (no *spin up* time), and require less power (more battery life).

The read/write speed for a standard HDD is usually in the region of 50 to 100 MB/s (usually closer to 50 MB). For SSDs, speeds are typically over 200 MB/s. For top-of-the-range models this can approach 500 MB/s. If you're wondering, read/write speeds for RAM are around 2 to 20 GB/s. So at best, SSDs are at least one order of magnitude slower than RAM, but still faster than standard HDDs.

If you are unsure about what type of hard drive you have, then time how long your computer takes to reach the login screen. If it is less than five seconds, you probably have an SSD.

Operating Systems: 32-Bit or 64-Bit

R comes in two versions: 32-bit and 64-bit. Your operating system also comes in two versions, 32-bit and 64-bit. Ideally, you want 64-bit versions of both R and the operating system. Using a 32-bit version of either has severe limitations on the amount of RAM R can access. So when we suggest that you should just buy more RAM, this assumes that you are using a 64-bit operating system, with a 64-bit version of R.

If you are using an OS version from the last five years, it is unlikely to be a 32-bit OS.

A 32-bit machine can access at most only 4 GB of RAM. Although some CPUs offer solutions to this limitation, if you are running a 32-bit operating system, then R is limited to around 3 GB of RAM. If you are running a 64-bit operating system but only a 32-bit version of R, then you have access to slightly more memory (but not much). Modern systems should run a 64-bit operating system, with a 64-bit version of R. Your memory limit is now measured as 8 TB for Windows machines and 128 TB for Unix-based OSes. An easy method for determining if you are running a 64-bit version of R is to run

```
.Machine$sizeof.pointer
```

which will return 8 if you a running a 64-bit version of R.

To find precise details, consult the R help pages `help("Memory-limits")` and `help("Memory")`.

Exercises

These exercises aim to condense the previous section into the key points.

1. Are you using a 32-bit or 64-bit version of R?

2. If you are using Windows, what are the results of running the command `mem ory.limit()`?

Central Processing Unit

The *central processing unit* (CPU), or the processor, is the brain of a computer. The CPU is responsible for performing numerical calculations. The faster the processor, the faster R will run. The clock speed (or clock rate, measured in hertz) is the frequency with which the CPU executes instructions. The faster the clock speed, the more instructions a CPU can execute in a section. CPU clock speed for a single CPU has been fairly static in the last couple of years, hovering around 3.4 GHz (see Figure 8-3).

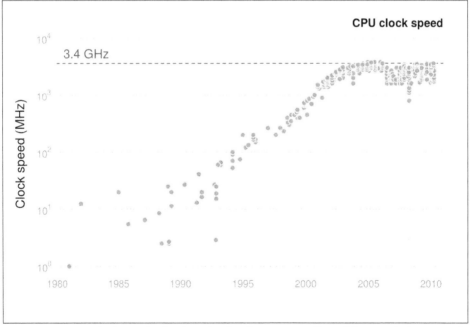

Figure 8-3. CPU clock speed. The data for this figure was collected from web-forum and Wikipedia. It is intended to indicate general trends in CPU speed.

Unfortunately, we can't simply use clock speeds to compare CPUs, since the internal architecture of a CPU plays a crucial role in determining its performance. The R package **benchmarkme** provides functions for benchmarking your system and contains data from previous benchmarks. Figure 8-4 shows the relative performance for over 150 CPUs.

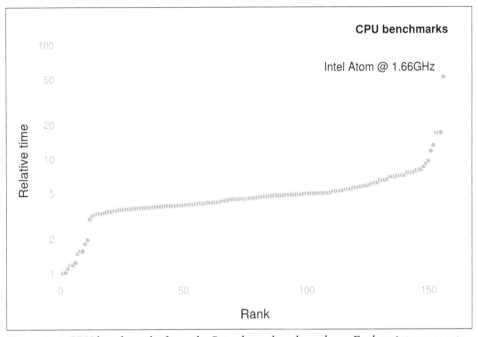

Figure 8-4. CPU benchmarks from the R package, benchmarkme. Each point represents an individual CPU result.

Running the benchmarks and comparing your CPU to others is straightforward using the **benchmarkme** package. After loading the package, we can benchmark your CPU

```
res = benchmark_std()
```

and compare the results to other users:

```
plot(res)
# Upload your benchmarks for future users
upload_results(res)
```

You get the model specifications of the top CPUs using `get_datatable(res)`.

Cloud Computing

Cloud computing uses networks of remote servers, instead of a local computer, to store and analyze data. It is now becoming increasingly popular to rent cloud computing resources.

Amazon EC2

Amazon Elastic Compute Cloud (EC2) is one of a number of providers of this service. EC2 makes it (relatively) easy to run R instances in the cloud. Users can configure the operating system, CPU, hard drive type, the amount of RAM, and where the project is physically located.

If you want to run a server in the Amazon EC2 cloud, you have to select the system you are going to boot up. There are a vast array of prepackaged system images. Some of these images are just basic operating systems, such as Debian or Ubuntu, which require further configuration. There is also an Amazon machine image (*http://www.louisaslett.com/RStudio_AMI/*) that specifically targets R and RStudio.

Exercise

1. To assess whether you should consider cloud computing, find out how much it would cost to rent a machine comparable to your laptop in the cloud for one year.

## CHAPTER 9

Efficient Collaboration

Large projects inevitably involve many people. This poses risks but also creates opportunities for improving computational efficiency and productivity, especially if project collaborators are reading and committing code. This chapter provides guidance on how to minimize the risks and maximize the benefits of collaborative R programming.

Collaborative working has a number of benefits. A team with a diverse skillset is usually stronger than a team with a very narrow focus. It makes sense to specialize: clearly defining roles such as statistician, frontend developer, system administrator, and project manager will make your team stronger. Even if you are working alone, dividing the work into discrete branches in this way can be useful, as discussed in Chapter 4.

Collaborative programming provides an opportunity for people to review each other's code. This can be encouraged by using a uniform style with many comments, as described in "Coding Style" on page 164. Like using a clear style in human language, following a style guide has the additional advantage of making your code more understandable to others.

When working on complex programming projects with multiple interdependencies, version control is essential. Even on small projects, tracking the progress of your project's code base has many advantages and makes collaboration much easier. Fortunately, it is now easier than ever before to integrate version control into your project, using RStudio's interface to the version control software `git` and online code-sharing websites such as GitHub. This is the subject of "Version Control" on page 169.

The final section, "Code Review" on page 173, addresses the question of working in a team and performing code reviews.

Prerequisites

This chapter deals with coding standards and techniques. The only packages required for this chapter are **lubridate** and **dplyr**. These packages are used to illustrate good practices.

Top Five Tips for Efficient Collaboration

1. Maintain a consistent coding style.

2. Think carefully about your comments and keep them up to date.

3. Use version control whenever possible.

4. Use informative commit messages.

5. Don't be afraid to elicit feedback from colleagues.

Coding Style

To be a successful programmer, you need to use a consistent programming style. There is no single *correct* style, but using multiple styles in the same project is wrong (Baath 2012). To some extent, good style is subjective and up to personal taste. There are, however, general principles that most programmers agree on, such as:

- Use modular code
- Comment your code
- Don't Repeat Yourself (DRY)
- Be concise, clear, and consistent

Good coding style will make you more efficient even if you are the only person who reads it. When your code is read by multiple readers or you are developing code with coworkers, having a consistent style is even more important. There are a number of R style guides online that are broadly similar, including one by Google (*https://google.github.io/styleguide/Rguide.xml*), Hadley Whickham (*http://adv-r.had.co.nz/Style.html*), and Richie Cotton (*http://bit.ly/Rcodestyle*). The style followed in this book is based on a combination of Hadley Wickham's guide and our own preferences (we follow Yihui Xie in preferring = to <- for assignment, for example).

In line with the principle of automation (automate any task that can save time by automating), the easiest way to improve your code is to ask your computer to do it using RStudio.

Reformatting Code with RStudio

RStudio can automatically clean up poorly indented and formatted code. To do this, select the lines that need to be formatted (e.g., via Ctrl-A to select the entire script), then automatically indent it with Ctrl-I. The shortcut Ctrl-Shift-A will reformat the code, adding spaces for maximum readability. An example is provided here:

```
# Poorly indented/formatted code
if(!exists("x")){
x=c(3,5)
y=x[2]}
```

This code chunk works but is not pleasant to read. RStudio automatically indents the code after the `if` statement as follows:

```
# Automatically indented code (Ctrl-I in RStudio)
if(!exists("x")){
  x=c(3,5)
  y=x[2]}
```

This is a start, but it's still not easy to read. This can be fixed in RStudio as illustrated in the following code chunk (these options can be seen in the Code menu, accessed with Alt-C on Windows/Linux computers):

```
# Automatically reformat the code (Ctrl-Shift-A in RStudio)
if(!exists("x")) {
  x = c(3, 5)
  y = x[2]
}
```

Note that some aspects of style are subjective; for example, we would not leave a space after the `if` and).

Filenames

Filenames should use the *.R* extension and should be lowercase (e.g., *load.R*). Avoid spaces. Use a dash or underscore to separate words.

```
# Good names
normalize.R
load.R
# Bad names
Normalize.r
load data.R
```

Section 1.1 of Writing R Extensions (*http://bit.ly/Rpackstructure*) provides more detailed guidance on filenames, such as avoiding non-English alphabetic characters as they cannot be guaranteed to work across locales. While the guidelines are strict, the guidance aids in making your scripts more portable.

Loading Packages

Library function calls should be at the top of your script. When loading an essential package, use `library` instead of `require` since a missing package will then raise an error. If a package isn't essential, use `require` and appropriately capture the warning raised. Package names should be surrounded with quotation marks.

```
# Good
library("dplyr")
# Non-standard evaluation
library(dplyr)
```

Avoid listing every package you may need; instead just include the packages you actually use. If you find that you are loading many packages, consider putting all packages in a file called *packages.R* and using `source` appropriately.

Commenting

Comments can greatly improve the efficiency of collaborative projects by helping everyone to understand what each line of code is doing. However, comments should be used carefully; plastering your script with comments does not necessarily make it more efficient, and too many comments can be inefficient. Updating heavily commented code can be a pain—not only will you have to change all the R code, you'll also have to rewrite or delete all the comments!

Ensure that your comments are meaningful. Avoid using verbose English to explain standard R code. The following comment, for example, adds no useful information because it is obvious by reading the code that i is being set to 1:

```
# Setting x equal to 1
x = 1
```

Instead, comments should provide context. Imagine that x was being used as a counter (in which case it should probably have a more meaningful name, like `counter`, but we'll continue to use x for illustrative purposes). In that case, the comment could explain your intention for its future use:

```
# Initialize counter
x = 1
```

The previous example illustrates that comments are more useful if they provide context and explain the programmer's intention (McConnell 2004). Each comment line should begin with a single hash (#), followed by a space. Comments can be toggled (turned on and off) in this way with Ctrl-Shift-C in RStudio. The double hash (##) can be reserved for R output. If you follow your comment with four dashes (# ----) RStudio will enable code folding until the next instance of this.

Object Names

> "When I use a word," Humpty Dumpty said, in a rather scornful tone, "it means just what I choose it to mean—neither more nor less."
>
> —Lewis Carroll, *Through the Looking Glass*, Chapter 6

It is important for objects and functions to be named consistently and sensibly. To take a silly example, imagine if all objects in your projects were called x, xx, xxx, etc. The code would run fine. However, it would be hard for other people, and a future you, to figure out what was going on, especially when you got to the object xxxxxxxxxx!

For this reason, giving a clear and consistent name to your objects, especially if they are going to be used many times in your script, can boost project efficiency (if an object is only used once, its name is less important, a case where x could be acceptable). Following discussion in "The State of Naming Conventions in R" (*http://bit.ly/ Rnamingcon*) by Rasmus Baath and elsewhere, we suggest an underscore_separated style for function and object names.[1] Unless you are creating an S3 object, avoid using a . in the name (this will help avoid confusing Python programmers!). Names should be concise yet meaningful.

In functions, the required arguments should always be first, followed by optional arguments. The special ... argument should come last. If your argument has a boolean value, use TRUE/FALSE instead of T/F for clarity.

 It's tempting to use T/F as shortcuts. But it is easy to accidentally redefine these variables (e.g., F = 10). R raises an error if you try to redefine TRUE/FALSE.

While it's possible to write arguments that depend on other arguments, try to avoid using this idiom as it makes understanding the default behavior harder to understand. Typically, it's easier to set an argument to have a default value of NULL and check its value using is.null() than by using missing(). Where possible, avoid using names of existing functions.

Example Package

The **lubridate** package is a good example of a package that has a consistent naming system, which makes it easy for users to guess its features and behavior. Dates are

---

1 One notable exception are packages in Bioconductor, where variable names are camelCase. In this case, you should match the existing style.

encoded in a variety of ways, but the `lubridate` package has a neat set of functions consisting of the three letters, *year*, *month*, and *day*. For example:

```
library("lubridate")
ymd("2012-01-02")
dmy("02-01-2012")
mdy("01-02-2012")
```

Assignment

The two most common ways of assigning objects to values in R is with `<-` and `=`. In most (but not all) contexts, they can be used interchangeably. Regardless of which operator you prefer, consistency is key, particularly when working in a group. In this book we use the `=` operator for assignment, as it's faster to type and more consistent with other languages.

The one place where a difference occurs is during function calls. Consider the following piece of code used for timing random number generation:

```
system.time(expr1 <- rnorm(10e5))
system.time(expr2 = rnorm(10e5)) # error
```

The first lines will run correctly *and* create a variable called `expr1`. The second line will raise an error. When we use `=` in a function call, it changes from an *assignment* operator to an *argument passing* operator. For further information about assignment, see `?assignOps`.

Spacing

Consistent spacing is an easy way of making your code more readable. Even a simple command such as `x = x + 1` takes a bit more time to understand when the spacing is removed (i.e., `x=x+1`). You should add a space around the operators `+`, `-`, `\`, and `*`. Include a space around the assignment operators, `<-` and `=`. Additionally, add a space around any comparison operators such as `==` and `<`. The latter rule helps avoid bugs:

```
# Bug. x now equals 1
x[x<-1]
# Correct. Selecting values less than -1
x[x < -1]
```

The exceptions to the space rule are `:`, `::`, and `:::`, as well as `$` and `@` symbols for selecting subparts of objects. As with English, add a space after a comma:

```
z[z$colA > 1990, ]
```

Indentation

Use two spaces to indent code. Never mix tabs and spaces. RStudio can automatically convert the tab character to spaces (see `Tools -> Global options -> Code`).

Curly Braces

Consider the following code:

```
# Bad style, fails
if(x < 5)
{
y}
else {
  x}
```

Typing this straight into R will result in an error. An opening curly brace, {, should not go on its own line and should always be followed by a line break. A closing curly brace should always go on its own line (unless it's followed by an else, in which case the else should go on its own line). The code inside curly braces should be indented (and RStudio will enforce this rule), as shown in the following code chunk:

```
# Good style
if(x < 5){
  x
} else {
  y
}
```

Exercise

1. Look at the difference between your style and RStudio's based on a representative R script that you have written (see "Coding Style" on page 164). What are the similarities? What are the differences? Are you consistent? Write these down and think about how you can use the results to improve your coding style.

Version Control

When a project gets large, complicated, or mission critical, it is important to keep track of how it evolves. In the same way that Dropbox saves a *backup* of your files, version control systems keep a backup of your code. The only difference is that version control systems back up your code *forever*.

The version control system we recommend is Git, a command-line application created by Linus Torvalds, who also invented Linux.[2] The easiest way to integrate your R projects with Git, if you're not accustomed to using a shell (e.g., the Unix command line), is with RStudio's Git tab in the top right-hand window (see Figure 9-1). This shows that a number of files have been modified (as illustrated with the blue M sym-

---

2 We recommend *10 Years of Git: An Interview with Git Creator Linus Torvalds* from Linux.com (*http://bit.ly/10yearsgit*) for more information on this topic.

bol) and that some are new (as illustrated with the yellow ? symbol). Checking the tick-box will enable these files to be *committed*.

Commits

Commits are the basic units of version control. Keep your commits *atomic*: each one should only do one thing. Document your work with clear and concise commit messages, and use the present tense (e.g., *add analysis functions*).

Committing code only updates the files on your *local* branch. To update the files stored on a remote server (e.g., on GitHub), you mush *push* the commit. This can be done using `git push` from a shell or using the green up arrow in RStudio, as illustrated in Figure 9-1. The blue down arrow will *pull* the latest version of the repository from the remote.[3]

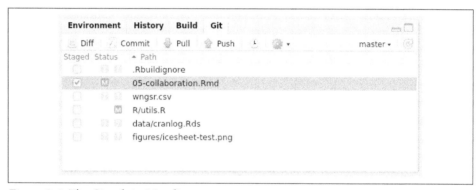

Figure 9-1. The Git tab in RStudio

Git Integration in RStudio

How do you enable this functionality on your installation of RStudio? RStudio can be a GUI Git only if Git has been installed *and* RStudio can find it. You need a working installation of Git (e.g., installed through `apt-get install git` Ubuntu/Debian or via GitHub Desktop (*http://bit.ly/installGHdesk*) for Mac and Windows). RStudio can be linked to your Git installation via Tools → Global Options in the Git/SVN tab. This tab also provides a link to a help page on RStudio/Git (*http://bit.ly/gitsvnrstudio*).

Once Git has been linked to your RStudio installation, it can be used to track changes in a new project by selecting `Create a git repository` when creating a new project. The tab illustrated in Figure 9-1 will appear, allowing functionality for interacting with Git via RStudio.

---

3 For a more detailed account of this process, see GitHub's help pages (*https://help.github.com/*).

RStudio provides a useful GUI for navigating past commits. This allows you to see the entire history of your project. To navigate and view the details of past commits, click on the Diff button in the Git pane, as illustrated in Figure 9-2.

Figure 9-2. The Git history navigation interface

GitHub

GitHub is an online platform that makes sharing your work and collaborating on code easy. There are alternatives such as GitLab (*https://about.gitlab.com/*). The focus here is on GitHub as it's by far the most popular among R developers. Also, through the command `devtools::install_github()`, preview versions of a package can be installed and updated in an instant. This makes *GitHub packages* a great way to access the latest functionality. And GitHub makes it easy to get your work *out there* to the world for efficiently collaborating with others, without the restraints placed on CRAN packages.

To install the GitHub version of the **benchmarkme** package, for example, you would enter

```
devtools::install_github("csgillespie/benchmarkme")
```

Note that `csgillespie` is the GitHub user and `benchmarkme` is the package name. Replacing `csgillespie` with `robinlovelace` in the previous code would install Robin's version of the package. This is useful for fast collaboration with many people, but you must remember that GitHub packages will not update automatically with the command `update.packages` (see "Updating R Packages" on page 24).

Although GitHub is fantastic for collaboration, it can end up creating more problems than it solves if your collaborators are not Git-literate. In one project, Robin eventually abandoned using GitHub after his collaborator found it impossible to work with. More time was being spent debugging Git/GitHub than actually working. Our advice therefore is to never impose Git and always ensure that other lines of communication (e.g., phone calls, emails) are open because different people prefer different ways of communicating.

Branches, Forks, Pulls, and Clones

Git is a large program that takes a long time to learn in-depth. However, getting to grips with the basics of some of its more advanced functions can make you a more efficient collaborator. Using and merging branches, for example, allows you to test new features in a self-contained environment before they are used in production (e.g., when shifting to an updated version of a package that is not backwards compatible). Instead of bogging you down with a comprehensive discussion of what is possible, this section cuts to the most important features for collaboration: branches, forks, pulls, and clones. For a more detailed description of Git's powerful functionality, we recommend the Jenny Bryan's book (*http://happygitwithr.com/*), *Happy Git and Git-Hub for the useR.*

Branches are distinct versions of your repository. Git allows you jump seamlessly between different versions of your entire project. To create a new branch called test, you need to enter the shell and use the Git command line:

```
git checkout -b test
```

This is equivalent to entering two commands: `git branch test` to create the branch and then `git checkout test` to *checkout* that branch. Checkout means switch into that branch. Any changes will not affect your previous branch. In RStudio, you can jump quickly between branches using the drop-down menu in the top right of the Git pane. This is illustrated in Figure 9-1: see the `master` text followed by a down arrow. Clicking on this will allow you to select other branches.

Forks are like branches, but they exist on other people's computers. You can fork a repository on GitHub easily, as described on the site's help pages (*https://help.github.com/articles/fork-a-repo/*). If you want an exact copy of this repository (including the commit history), you can *clone* this fork to your computer using the command `git clone` or by using a Git GUI such as GitHub Desktop. This is preferable from a collaboration perspective than cloning the repository directly, because any changes can be pushed back online easily if you are working from your own fork. You cannot push to forks that you have not created, unless someone has granted you access. If you want your work to be incorporated into the original fork, you can use a *pull request*. Note: if you don't need the project's entire commit history, you can simply download a zip file containing the latest version of the repository from GitHub (at the top right of any GitHub repository).

A *pull request* (PR) is a mechanism on GitHub by which your code can be added to an existing project. One of the most useful features of a PR from a collaboration perspective is that it provides an opportunity for others to comment on your code, line by line, before it gets merged. This is all done online on GitHub, as discussed in GitHub's online help (*https://help.github.com/articles/merging-a-pull-request/*). Following feedback, you may want to refactor code written by you or others.

Code Review

What is a code review?[4] Simply put, when we have finished working on a piece of code, a colleague reviews our work and considers questions such as:

- Is the code correct and properly documented?
- Could the code be improved?
- Does the code conform to existing style guidelines?
- Are there any automated tests? If so, are they sufficient?

A good code review shares knowledge and best practices.

A lightweight code review can take a variety of forms. For example, it could be as simple as emailing around some code for comments, or "over the shoulder," where someone literally looks over your shoulder while you code. More formal techniques include paired programming where two developers work side by side on the same project.

Regardless of the review method being employed, there a number of points to remember. First, as with all forms of feedback, be constructive. Rather than pointing out flaws, give suggested improvements. Closely related is giving praise when appropriate. Second, if you are reviewing a piece of code, set a timeframe or the number of lines of code you will review. For example, you will spend one hour to review a piece of code, or review a maximum of 400 lines. Third, a code review should be performed before the code is merged into a larger code base; fix mistakes as soon as possible.

Many R users don't work on a team or in a group; instead, they work by themselves. Practically, there isn't usually anyone nearby to review their code. However, there is still the option of an *unoffical* code review. For example, if you have hosted code on an online repository such as GitHub, users will naturally give feedback on our code

---

4 This section is being written with small teams in mind. Larger teams should consult a more detailed text on code review.

(especially if you make it clear that you welcome feedback). Another good place is Stack Overflow (covered in detail in Chapter 10). This site allows you to post answers to other users questions. When you post an answer, if your code is unclear, this will be flagged in comments below your answer.

References

Bååth, Rasmus. 2012. "The State of Naming Conventions in R." *The R Journal* 4 (2): 74–75. *https://journal.r-project.org/archive/2012-2/RJournal_2012-2_Baaaath.pdf.*

McConnell, Steve. 2004. *Code Complete.* Pearson Education.

## CHAPTER 10

Efficient Learning

As with any vibrant open source software community, R is fast moving. This can be disorienting because it means that you can never *finish* learning R. On the other hand, it makes R a fascinating subject because there is always more to learn. Even experienced R users keep finding new functionality that helps solve problems more quickly and elegantly. Therefore, *learning how to learn* is one of the most important skills to have if you want to learn R *in-depth*. We emphasize *depth* of learning because it is more efficient to learn something properly than to Google it repeatedly every time you forget how it works.

This chapter aims to equip you with concepts, guidance, and tips that will accelerate your transition from an R *hacker* to an R *programmer*. This inevitably involves effective use of R's help, reading R source code, and use of online material.

Prerequisties

The only package used in this section is **swirl**:

```
library("swirl")
```

Top Five Tips for Efficient Learning

1. Use R's internal help (e.g., with ?, ??, `vignette()`, and `apropos()`). Try **swirl**.

2. Read about the latest developments in established outlets such as the *Journal for Statistical Software*, the *R Journal*, R lists, and the *blogosphere*.

3. If stuck, ask for help! A clear question posted in an appropriate place, using reproducible code, should get a quick and enlightening answer.

4. For more in-depth learning, nothing can beat immersive R books and tutorials. Do some research and decide which resources you should use.

5. One of the best ways to consolidate learning is to write it up and pass on the knowledge; telling the story of what you've learned with also help others.

Using R's Internal Help

Sometimes the best place to look for help is within R itself. Using R's help has three main advantages from an efficiency perspective:

- It's faster to query R from inside your IDE than to switch context and search for help on a different platform (e.g., the internet, which has countless distractions).

- It works offline.

- Learning to read R's documentation (and source code) is a powerful skill in itself that will improve your R programming.

The main disadvantage of R's internal help is that it is terse and in some cases sparse. Do not expect to *always* be able to find the answer in R, so be prepared to look elsewhere for more detailed help and context. From a learning perspective, becoming acquainted with R's documentation is often better than finding the solution from a different source because it was written by developers, largely for developers. Therefore, with R documentation you learn about functions *from the horse's mouth*. R help also sometimes sheds light on a function's history through references to academic papers.

As you look to learn about a topic or function in R, it is likely that you will have a search strategy of your own, ranging from broad to narrow:

1. Searching R and installed packages for help on a specific *topic*.

2. Reading up on *packages* vignettes.

3. Getting help on a specific *function*.

4. Looking into the *source code*.

In many cases, you may already have gone through stages 1 and 2. Often you can stop at stage 3 and simply use the function without worrying about exactly how it works. In every case, it is useful to be aware of this hierarchical approach to learning from R's internal help, so you can start with the *big picture* (and avoid going down a misguided route early on) and then quickly focus in on the functions that are most related to your task.

To illustrate this approach in action, imagine that you are interested in a specific topic: optimization. The remainder of this section will work through stages 1 to 4 outlined previously as if we wanted to find out more about this topic, with occasional diversions from it to see how specific help functions work in more detail. The final method of learning from R's internal resources covered in this section is **swirl**, a package for interactive learning.

Searching R for Topics

A *wide boundary* search for a topic in R will often begin with a search for instances of a keyword in the documentation and function names. Using the example of optimization, you could start with a search for a text string related to the topic of interest:

```
# help.search("optim") # or, more concisely
??optim
```

Note that the `??` symbol is simply a useful shorthand version of the function `help.search()`. It is sometimes useful to use the full function rather than the shorthand version, because it allows you to specify a number of options. To search for all help pages that mention the more specific term "optimization" in the title or alias of the help pages, for example, the following command would be used:

```
help.search(pattern = "optimisation|optimization",
    fields = c("title", "concept"))
```

This will return a short (and potentially more efficiently focused) list of help pages than the wide-ranging `??optim` call. To make the search even more specific, we can use the `package` argument to constrain the search to a single package. This can be very useful when you know that a function exists in a specific package but you cannot remember what it is called:

```
help.search(pattern = "optimisation|optimization",
    fields = c("title", "concept"), package = "stats")
```

Another function for searching R is `apropos()`. It prints to the console any R objects (including *hidden* functions, those beginning with ., and datasets) whose name matches a given text string. Because it does not search R's documentation, it tends to return fewer results than `help.search()`. Its use and typical outputs can be seen in the following examples:

```
apropos("optim")
#> [1] "constrOptim" "optim"        "optimHess"   "optimise"    "optimize"
apropos("lm")[1:6] # show only first six results
#> [1] ".__C__anova.glm"      ".__C__anova.glm.null" ".__C__diagonalMatrix"
#> [4] ".__C__generalMatrix"  ".__C__glm"            ".__C__glm.null"
```

To search *all R packages*, including those you have not installed locally, for a specific topic, there are a number of options. For obvious reasons, this requires internet access. The most rudimentary way to see what packages are available from CRAN, if you are using RStudio, is to use its autocompletion functionality for package names. To take an example, if you are looking for a package for geospatial data analysis, you could do worse than enter the text string geo as an argument into package installation function (e.g., install.packages(geo)) and pressing the Tab key when the cursor is between the o and the) in the example. The resulting options are shown in Figure 10-1. Selecting one from the drop-down menu will result in it being completed with surrounding quotation marks, as necessary.

Figure 10-1. Package name autocompletion in action in RStudio for packages beginning with geo

Finding and Using Vignettes

Some packages contain vignettes. These are pieces of *long-form* documentation (*http://r-pkgs.had.co.nz/vignettes.html*) that allow package authors to go into detail explaining how the package works (Wickham 2015c). In general, they are high quality. Because they can be used to illustrate real-world use cases, vignettes can be the best way to understand functions in the context of broader explanations and longer examples than are provided in function help pages. Although many packages lack vignettes, they deserve a subsection of their own because they can boost the efficiency with which package functions are used in an integrated workflow.

 If you are frustrated because a certain package lacks a vignette, you can create one. This can be a great way of learning about and consolidating your knowledge of a package. To create a vignette, first download the source code of a package and then use dev tools::use_vignette(). To add a vignette to the **efficient** package used in this book, for example, you could clone the repo (e.g., using the command git clone git@github.com:csgillespie/effi cient). Once you have opened the repo as a project (e.g., in RStudio), you could create a vignette called "efficient-learning" with the command use_vignette("efficient-learning").

To browse any vignettes associated with a particular package, we can use the handy function browseVignettes():

```
browseVignettes(package = "benchmarkme")
```

This is roughly equivalent to `vignette(package = "benchmarkme")` but opens a new page in a browser and lets you navigate all the vignettes in that particular package. For an overview of all vignettes available from R packages installed on your computer, try browsing all available vignettes with `browseVignettes()`. You may be surprised at how many hidden gems there are in there!

How best to *use* vignettes depends on the vignette in question and your aims. In general, you should expect to spend longer reading vignettes than other types of R documentation. The *Introduction to dplyr* vignette (opened with `vignette("introduction", package = "dplyr")`), for example, contains almost 4,000 words of prose, example code, and outputs that illustrate how its functions work. We recommend working through the examples and typing the example code in order to *learn by doing*.

Another way to learn from package vignettes is to view their source code. You can find where vignette source code lives by looking in the `vignette/` folder of the package's source code. **dplyr**'s vignettes, for example, can be viewed (and edited) online (*https://github.com/hadley/dplyr/tree/master/vignettes*). A quick way to view a vignette's R code is with the `edit()` function:

```
v = vignette("introduction", package = "dplyr")
edit(v)
```

Getting Help on Functions

All functions have help pages. These contain, at a minimum, a list of the input arguments and the nature of the output that can be expected. Once a function has been identified (e.g., using one of the methods outlined in "Searching R for Topics" on page 177), its help page can be displayed by prefixing the function name with ?. Continuing with the previous example, the help page associated with the command `optim()` (for general-purpose optimization) can be invoked as follows:

```
# help("optim") # or, more concisely:
?optim
```

In general, help pages describe *what* functions do, not *how* they work. This is one of the reasons that function help pages are thought (by some) to be difficult to understand. In practice, this means that the help page does not describe the underlying mathematics or algorithm in detail—its aim is to describe the interface.

A help page is divided into a number of sections. The help for `optim()` is typical in that it has a title (general-purpose optimization) followed by short Description, Usage, and Arguments sections. The Description is usually just a sentence or two explaining what it does. Usage shows the arguments that the function needs to work. And Arguments describes what kind of objects the function expects. Longer sections typically include Details and Examples, which provide some context and provide (usually reproducible) examples of how the function can be used, respectively. The typically short Value, References, and See Also sections facilitate efficient learning by explaining what the output means, where you can find academic literature on the subject, and related functions.

`optim()` is a mature and heavily used function so it has a long help page; you'll probably be glad to know that not all help pages are this long! With so much potentially overwhelming information in a single help page, the placement of the short, dense sections at the beginning is efficient because it helps you to understand the fundamentals of a function in few words. Learning how to read and quickly interpret such help pages will greatly help your ability to learn R. Take some time to study the help for `optim()` in detail.

It is worth discussing the contents of the Usage section in particular, because this contains information that may not be immediately obvious:

```
optim(par, fn, gr = NULL, ...,
      method = c("Nelder-Mead", "BFGS", "CG", "L-BFGS-B", "SANN", "Brent"),
      lower = -Inf, upper = Inf, control = list(), hessian = FALSE)
```

This contains two pieces of critical information:

1. The *essential* arguments that must be provided for the function to work (par and fn in this case, as gr has a default value) before the ... symbol; and

2. *optional* arguments that control how the function works (method, lower, and hessian in this case). ... are optional arguments whose values depend on the other arguments (which will be passed to the function represented by fn in this case). Let's see how this works in practice by trying to run `optim()` to find the minimum value of the function $y = x^4 - x^2$:

```
fn = function(x) {
  x^4 - x^2
}
optim(par = 0, fn = fn)
#> Warning in optim(par = 0, fn = fn): one-dimensional optimization
#> by Nelder-Mead is unreliable: use "Brent" or optimize() directly
#> $par
#> [1] 0.707
#>
#> $value
#> [1] -0.25
#>
#> $counts
#> function gradient
#>       58       NA
#>
#> $convergence
```

```
#> [1] 0
#>
#> $message
#> NULL
```

The results show that the minimum value of fn(x) is found when x = 0.707.. (1 / √2), with a minimum value of -0.25. It took 58 iterations of the function call for optim() to converge on this value. Each of these output values is described in the Values section of the help pages. From the help pages, we could guess that providing the function call without specifying par (i.e., optim(fn = fn)) would fail, which indeed it does.

The most *helpful* section is often the Examples. These lie at the bottom of the help page and show precisely how the function works. You can either copy and paste the code, or actually run the example code using the example command (it is well worth running these examples due to the graphics produced):

```
example(optim)
```

When a package is added to CRAN, the example part of the documentation is run on all major platforms. This helps ensure that a package works on multiple systems.

Another useful section in the help file is See Also:. In the optim() help page, it links to optimize(), which may be more appropriate for this use case.

Reading R Source Code

R is open source. This means that we view the underlying source code and examine any function. Of course the code is complex, and diving straight into the source code won't help that much. However, watching the GitHub R source code mirror (*https://github.com/wch/r-source/*) will allow you to monitor small changes that occur. This gives a nice entry point into a complex code base. Likewise, examining the source of small functions such as NCOL is informative (e.g., getFunction("NCOL")).

Subscribing to the R NEWS blog (*https://developer.r-project.org/blosxom.cgi/R-devel/NEWS/*) is an easy way of keeping track of future changes.

Many R packages are developed in the open on GitHub or r-forge. Select a few well-known packages and examine their sources. A good package to start with is **drat** (*https://github.com/eddelbuettel/drat*). This is a relatively simple package developed by

Dirk Eddelbuettel (author of **Rcpp**) that only contains a few functions. It gives you an excellent pointer into software development by one of the key R package writers.

A shortcut for browsing R's source code is provided by the RStudio IDE: clicking on a function and then pressing the F2 key will open its source code in the file editor. This works both for functions that exist in R and its packages and functions that you created in another R script (so long as it is within your project directory). Although reading source code can be interesting in itself, it is probably best done in the context of a specific question, such as "how can I use a function name as an argument in my own function?" (looking at the source code of apply() may help here).

swirl

swirl is an interactive teaching platform for R. It offers a number of extensions and, for the pioneering, the ability for others to create custom extensions. The learning curve and method will not work for everyone, but this package is worth flagging as a potent self-teaching resource. In some ways, **swirl** can be seen as the ultimate internal R help as it allows dedicated learning sessions, based on multiple choice questions, all within a usual R session. To enter the **swirl** world, just enter the following. The resultant instructions will explain the rest:

```
library("swirl")
swirl()
```

Online Resources

The R community has a strong online presence, providing many resources for learning. Over time, there has fortunately been a tendency for R resources to become more user friendly and up-to-date. Many resources that have been on CRAN for many years are dated by now so it's more efficient to navigate directly to the most up-to-date and efficient-to-use resources.

Cheat sheets are short documents summarizing how to do certain things. RStudio (*http://www.rstudio.com/resources/cheatsheets/*), for example, provides excellent cheat sheets on **dplyr** (*http://bit.ly/dplyrcheatsheet*), **rmarkdown** (*http://bit.ly/rmdcheatsheet*), and the RStudio IDE (*http://bit.ly/rstudioidecheatsheet*) itself.

The R-project website contains six detailed official manuals (*https://cran.r-project.org/manuals.html*), plus a giant PDF file containing documentation for all recommended packages. These include An Introduction to R (*http://bit.ly/introtoR*), The R Language Definition (*http://bit.ly/Rlangdef*), and R Installation and Administration (*http://bit.ly/Rinstalladmin*), all of which are recommended for people wanting to learn general R skills. If you are developing a package and want to submit it to CRAN, the Writing R Extensions (*http://bit.ly/writingRextensions*) manual is recommended reading, although it has to some extent been superseded by *R Packages* by Hadley Wickham (O'Reilly), the source code of which is available online (*https://github.com/hadley/r-pkgs*). While these manuals are long, they contain important information written by experienced R programmers.

For more domain-specific and up-to-date information on developments in R, we recommend checking out academic journals. The R Journal (*https://journal.r-project.org/*) regularly publishes articles describing new R packages, as well as general programming hints. Similarly, the articles in the Journal of Statistical Software (*https://www.jstatsoft.org/*) have a strong R bias. Publications in these journals are generally of very high quality and have been rigorously peer reviewed. However, they may be rather technical for R novices.

The wider community provides a much larger body of information, of more variable quality, than the official R resources. The Contributed Documentation (*https://cran.r-project.org/other-docs.html*) page on R's home page contains dozens of tutorials and other resources on a wide range of topics. Some of these are excellent, although many are not kept up-to-date. An excellent resource for browsing R help pages online is provided by rdocumentation.org.

Lower grade but more frequently released information can be found on the *blogosphere*. Central to this is R-bloggers (*http://www.r-bloggers.com/*), a blog aggregator of content contributed by bloggers who write about R (in English). It is a great way to get exposed to new and different packages. Similarly, monitoring the *#rstats* (*http://bit.ly/rstatshashtag*) Twitter tag keeps you up-to-date with the latest news.

There are also mailing lists, Google groups, and the Stack Exchange Q&A sites. Before requesting help, read a few other questions to learn the format of the site. Make sure you search previous questions so you are not duplicating work. Perhaps the most important point is to remember that people aren't under any obligation to answer your question. One of the fantastic things about the open source community is that you can ask questions and one of core developers may answer your question for free—but remember, everyone is busy!

Stack Overflow

The number one place on the internet for getting help on programming is Stack Overflow (*http://www.stackoverflow.com*). This website provides a platform for asking and answering questions. Through site membership, questions and answers are voted up or down. Users of Stack Overflow earn reputation points when their question or answer is up-voted. Anyone (with enough reputation) can edit a question or answer. This helps the content remain relevant.

Questions are tagged. The R questions can be found under the R tag (*http://stackoverflow.com/questions/tagged/r*). The R page (*https://stackoverflow.com/tags/r/info*) contains links to official documentation, free resources, and various other links.

Members of the Stack Overflow R community have tagged, using `r-faq`, a few question that often crop up.

Mailing Lists and Groups

There are many mailing lists and Google groups focused on R and particular packages. The main list for getting help is `R-help`. This is a high-volume mailing list, with around a dozen messages per day. A more technical mailing list is `R-devel`. This list is intended for questions and discussion about code development in R. The discussion on this list is very technical. It's a good place to be introduced to new ideas, but it's not the place to ask about these ideas! There are many other special-interest mailing lists (*https://www.r-project.org/mail.html*) covering topics such as high-performance computing to ecology. Many popular packages also have their own mailing list or Google group (e.g., **ggplot2** and **shiny**). The key piece of advice is before mailing a list, read the relevant mailing archive and check that your message is appropriate.

Asking a Question

A great way to get specific help on a difficult topic is to ask for help. However, asking a good question is not easy. Three common mistakes, and ways to avoid them, are outlined here:

1. Asking a question that has already been asked; make sure that you've properly searched for the answer before posting.

2. The answer to the question can be found in R's help: make sure that you've properly read the relevant help pages before asking.

3. The question does not contain a reproducible example; create a simple version of your data, show the code you've tried, and display the result you are hoping for.

Your question should contain just enough information that your problem is clear and can be reproducible, while at the same time avoids unnecessary details. Fortunately there is a Stack Overflow question—How to make a great R reproducible example? (*http://bit.ly/Rreproducible*)—that provides excellent guidance. Additional guides that explain how to create good programming questions are provided by Stack Overflow (*https://stackoverflow.com/help/how-to-ask*) and the R mailing list posting guide (*https://www.r-project.org/posting-guide.html*).

Minimal Dataset

What is the smallest dataset you can construct that will reproduce your issue? Your actual dataset may contain 10^5 rows and 10^4 columns, but to get your idea across you might only need four rows and three columns. Making small example datasets is easy.

For example, to create a data frame with two numeric columns and a column of characters, use the following:

```
set.seed(1)
example_df = data.frame(x = rnorm(4), y = rnorm(4), z = sample(LETTERS, 4))
```

Note that the call to set.seed ensures that anyone who runs the code will get the same random number stream. Alternatively, you can use one of the many datasets that come with R - library(help = "datasets").

If creating an example dataset isn't possible, then use dput on your actual dataset. This will create an ASCII text representation of the object that will enable anyone to recreate the object:

```
dput(example_df)
#> structure(list(
#>   x = c(-0.626453810742332, 0.183643324222082, -0.835628612410047,
#>   1.59528080213779),
#>   y = c(0.329507771815361, -0.820468384118015, 0.487429052428485,
#>   0.738324705129217),
#>   z = structure(c(3L, 4L, 1L, 2L), .Label = c("J", "R", "S", "Y"),
#>   class = "factor")),
#>   .Names = c("x", "y", "z"), row.names = c(NA, -4L), class = "data.frame")
```

Minimal Example

What you should not do is simply copy and paste your entire function into your question. It's unlikely that your entire function doesn't work, so just simplify it to the bare minimum. The aim is to target your actual issue. Avoid copying and pasting large blocks of code; remove superfluous lines that are not part of the problem. Before asking your question, can you run your code in a clean R environment and reproduce your error?

Learning In Depth

In the age of the internet and social media, many people feel lucky if they have time to go for a walk, let alone sit down to read a book. But it is undeniable that learning R *in depth* is a time-consuming activity. Reading a book or a large tutorial (and completing the practical examples contained within) may not be the most efficient way to solve a particular problem in the short term, but it can be one of the best ways to learn R programming properly, especially in the long run.

In-depth learning differs from shallow, incremental learning because rather than discovering how a specific function works, you find out how systems of functions work together. To take a metaphor from civil engineering, in-depth learning is about building strong foundations on which a wide range of buildings can be constructed. In-depth learning can be highly efficient in the long run because it will pay back over many years, regardless of the domain-specific problem you want to use R to tackle. Shallow learning, to continue the metaphor, is more like erecting many temporary structures: they can solve a specific problem in the short term, but they will not be durable. Flimsy dwellings can be swept away. Shallow memories can be forgotten.

Having established that time spent *deep learning* can, counterintuitively, be efficient, it is worth thinking about how to deep learn. This varies from person to person. It does not involve passively absorbing sacred information transmitted year after year by the *R gods*. It is an active, participatory process. To ensure that memories are rapidly actionable you must *learn by doing*. Learning from a cohesive, systematic, and relatively comprehensive resource will help you to see the many interconnections between the different elements of R programming and how they can be combined for efficient work.

There are a number of such resources, including this book. Although the understandable tendency will be to use it incrementally, dipping in and out of different sections when different problems arise, we also recommend reading it systematically to see how the different elements of efficiency fit together. It is likely that as you work progressively through this book, in parallel with solving real-world problems, you will realize that the solution is not to have the *right* resource at hand but to be able to use the tools provided by R efficiently. Once you hit this level of proficiency, you should have the confidence to address most problems encountered from first principles. Over time, your *first port of call* should move away from Google and even R's internal help to simply giving it a try. Informed trial and error, and intelligent experimentation, can be the best approach to both learning and solving problems quickly, once you are equipped with the tools to do so. That's why this is the last section in the book.

If you have already worked through all the examples in this book, or if you want to learn areas not covered in it, there are many excellent resources for extending and deepening your knowledge of R programming for fast and effective work, and to do new things with it. Because R is a large and ever-evolving language, there is no definitive list of resources for taking your R skills to new heights. However, the following list, in rough ascending order of difficulty and depth, should provide plenty of material and motivation for in-depth learning of R.

1. Free webinars and online courses provided by RStudio (*http://www.rstudio.com/ resources/webinars/*) and DataCamp (*https://www.datacamp.com/community/ open-courses*). Both organizations are well regarded and keep their content up-to-date, but there are likely other sources of other online courses. We recommend that you test pushing your abilities, rather than going over the same material covered in this book.

2. *R for Data Science* (Grolemund and Wickham 2016), a free book introducing many concepts and *tidy* packages for working with data (a free online version is available from *r4ds.had.co.nz*).

3. *R Programming for Data Science* (Peng 2014), which provides in-depth coverage of analysis and visualization of datasets.

4. *Advanced R Programming* (Wickham 2014a), an advanced book that looks at the internals of how R works (free from *adv-r.had.co.nz*).

Spread the Knowledge

The final thing to say on the topic of efficient learning relates to the old (~2000 years old!) saying *docendo discimus* (*https://en.wikipedia.org/wiki/Docendo_discimus*):

> by teaching we learn

This means that passing on information is one of the best ways to consolidate your learning. It was largely by helping others learn R that we became proficient R users.

Demand for R skills is growing, so there are many opportunities to teach R. Whether it's helping your colleague use `apply()` or writing a blog post on solving certain problems in R, teaching others R can be a rewarding experience. Furthermore, spreading the knowledge can be efficient: it will improve your own understanding of the language and benefit the entire community, providing positive feedback to the movement toward open source software in data-driven computing.

Assuming you have completed this book, the only remaining thing to say is "Well done! You are now an efficient R programmer." We hope you direct your newly found skills toward the greater good and pass on the wisdom to others along the way.

References

Wickham, Hadley. 2015c. *R Packages*. O'Reilly Media.

Grolemund, G., and H. Wickham. 2016. *R for Data Science*. O'Reilly Media.

Peng, Roger. 2014. *R Programming for Data Science*. Leanpub. *https://leanpub.com/rprogramming*.

Wickham, Hadley. 2014a. *Advanced R*. CRC Press.

Package Dependencies

The book uses datasets stored in the **efficient** GitHub package, which can be installed (after **devtools** has been installed) as follows:

```
devtools::install_github("csgillespie/efficient",
                         args = "--with-keep.source")
```

The book depends on the following CRAN packages:

Name	Title	Version
assertive.reflection	Assertions for Checking the State of R (Cotton 2016a)	0.0.3
benchmarkme	Crowd Sourced System Benchmarks (Gillespie 2016)	0.3.0
bookdown	Authoring Books with R Markdown (Xie 2016a)	0.1
cranlogs	Download Logs from the *RStudio CRAN* Mirror (Csardi 2015)	2.1.0
data.table	Extension of Data.frame (Dowle et al. 2015)	1.9.6
devtools	Tools to Make Developing R Packages Easier (H. Wickham and Chang 2016a)	1.12.0
DiagrammeR	Create Graph Diagrams and Flowcharts Using R (Sveidqvist et al. 2016)	0.8.4
dplyr	A Grammar of Data Manipulation (Wickham and Francois 2016)	0.5.0
drat	Drat R Archive Template (Carl Boettiger et al. 2016)	0.1.1
efficient	Becoming an Efficient R Programmer (Gillespie and Lovelace 2016)	0.1.1
feather	R Bindings to the Feather *API* (H. Wickham 2016a)	0.3.0
formatR	Format R Code Automatically (Xie 2016b)	1.4
fortunes	R Fortunes (Zeileis and R community 2016)	1.5.3
geosphere	Spherical Trigonometry (Hijmans 2016)	1.5.5
ggmap	Spatial Visualization with ggplot2 (Kahle and Wickham 2016)	2.6.1
ggplot2	An Implementation of the Grammar of Graphics (H. Wickham and Chang 2016b)	2.1.0
ggplot2movies	Movies Data (H. Wickham 2015a)	0.0.1
knitr	A General-Purpose Package for Dynamic Report Generation in R (Xie 2016c)	1.14

Name	Title	Version
lubridate	Make Dealing with Dates a Little Easier (Grolemund, Spinu, and Wickham 2016)	1.5.6
microbenchmark	Accurate Timing Functions (Mersmann 2015)	1.4.2.1
profvis	Interactive Visualizations for Profiling R Code (Chang and Luraschi 2016)	0.3.2
pryr	Tools for Computing on the Language (H. Wickham 2015b)	0.1.2
Rcpp	Seamless R and C++ Integration (Eddelbuettel et al. 2016)	0.12.7
readr	Read Tabular Data (Wickham, Hester, and Francois 2016)	1.0.0
rio	A Swiss-Army Knife for Data I/O (Chan and Leeper 2016)	0.4.12
RSQLite	SQLite Interface for R (Wickham, James, and Falcon 2014)	1.0.0
tibble	Simple Data Frames (Wickham, Francois, and Müller 2016)	1.2
tidyr	Easily Tidy Data with `spread()` and `gather()` Functions (H. Wickham 2016b)	0.6.0

References

Bååth, Rasmus. 2012. "The State of Naming Conventions in R." The *R Journal* 4 (2): 74–75. *https://journal.r-project.org/archive/2012-2/RJournal_2012-2_Baaaath.pdf.*

Berkun, Scott. 2005. *The Art of Project Management*. O'Reilly Media.

Braun, John, and Duncan J Murdoch. 2007. *A First Course in Statistical Programming with R*. Vol. 25. Cambridge University Press Cambridge.

Burns, Patrick. 2011. *The R Inferno*. Lulu.com.

Carl Boettiger, Dirk Eddelbuettel with contributions by, Sebastian Gibb, Colin Gillespie, Jan Górecki, Matt Jones, Thomas Leeper, Steven Pav, and Jan Schulz. 2016. *Drat: Drat R Archive Template. https://CRAN.R-project.org/package=drat.*

Chan, Chung-hong, and Thomas J. Leeper. 2016. *Rio: A Swiss-Army Knife for Data I/O. https://CRAN.R-project.org/package=rio.*

Chang, Winston. 2012. *R Graphics Cookbook*. O'Reilly Media.

Chang, Winston, and Javier Luraschi. 2016. *Profvis: Interactive Visualizations for Profiling R Code. https://CRAN.R-project.org/package=profvis.*

Codd, E. F. 1979. "Extending the database relational model to capture more meaning." ACM Transactions on Database Systems 4 (4): 397–434. doi:10.1145/320107.320109 (*https://doi.org/10.1145/320107.320109*).

Cotton, Richard. 2013. *Learning R*. O'Reilly Media.

———. 2016a. *Assertive.reflection: Assertions for Checking the State of R. https://CRAN.R-project.org/package=assertive.reflection.*

———. 2016b. *Testing R Code.*

Csardi, Gabor. 2015. *Cranlogs: Download Logs from the 'RStudio' 'CRAN' Mirror*. *https://CRAN.R-project.org/package=cranlogs*.

Dowle, M, A Srinivasan, T Short, S Lianoglou with contributions from R Saporta, and E Antonyan. 2015. *Data.table: Extension of Data.frame*. *https://CRAN.R-project.org/package=data.table*.

Eddelbuettel, Dirk. 2013. *Seamless R and C++ Integration with Rcpp*. Springer.

Eddelbuettel, Dirk, and Romain François. 2011. "Rcpp: Seamless R and C++ Integration." *Journal of Statistical Software* 40 (8): 1–18.

Eddelbuettel, Dirk, Romain Francois, JJ Allaire, Kevin Ushey, Qiang Kou, Douglas Bates, and John Chambers. 2016. *Rcpp: Seamless R and C++ Integration*. *https://CRAN.R-project.org/package=Rcpp*.

Eddelbuettel, Dirk, Romain François, J. Allaire, John Chambers, Douglas Bates, and Kevin Ushey. 2011. "Rcpp: Seamless R and C++ Integration." *Journal of Statistical Software* 40 (8): 1–18.

Eddelbuettel, Dirk, Murray Stokely, and Jeroen Ooms. 2016. "RProtoBuf: Efficient Cross-Language Data Serialization in R." *Journal of Statistical Software* 71 (1): 1–24. doi:10.18637/jss.v071.i02.

Gillespie, Colin. 2016. *Benchmarkme: Crowd Sourced System Benchmarks*. *https://CRAN.R-project.org/package=benchmarkme*.

Gillespie, Colin, and Robin Lovelace. 2016. *Efficient: Becoming an Efficient R Programmer*.

Goldberg, David. 1991. "What Every Computer Scientist Should Know About Floating-Point Arithmetic." *ACM Computing Surveys (CSUR)* 23 (1). ACM: 5–48.

Grant, Christine A, Louise M Wallace, and Peter C Spurgeon. 2013. "An Exploration of the Psychological Factors Affecting Remote E-Worker's Job Effectiveness, Well-Being and Work-Life Balance." *Employee Relations* 35 (5). Emerald Group Publishing Limited: 527–46.

Grolemund, G., and H. Wickham. 2016. *R for Data Science*. O'Reilly Media.

Grolemund, Garrett, Vitalie Spinu, and Hadley Wickham. 2016. *Lubridate: Make Dealing with Dates a Little Easier*. *https://CRAN.R-project.org/package=lubridate*.

Hijmans, Robert J. 2016. *Geosphere: Spherical Trigonometry*. *https://CRAN.R-project.org/package=geosphere*.

Janert, Philipp K. 2010. *Data Analysis with Open Source Tools*. "O'Reilly Media".

Jensen, Jørgen Dejgård. 2011. "Can Worksite Nutritional Interventions Improve Productivity and Firm Profitability? A Literature Review." *Perspectives in Public Health* 131 (4). SAGE Publications: 184–92.

Kahle, David, and Hadley Wickham. 2016. *Ggmap: Spatial Visualization with Ggplot2.* *https://CRAN.R-project.org/package=ggmap.*

Kersten, Martin L, Stratos Idreos, Stefan Manegold, Erietta Liarou, and others. 2011. "The Researcher's Guide to the Data Deluge: Querying a Scientific Database in Just a Few Seconds." *PVLDB Challenges and Visions* 3.

Kruchten, Philippe, Robert L Nord, and Ipek Ozkaya. 2012. "Technical Debt: From Metaphor to Theory and Practice." *IEEE Software*, no. 6. IEEE: 18–21.

Lovelace, Ada Countess. 1842. "Translators notes to an article on Babbages Analytical Engine." *Scientific Memoirs* 3. 691-731.

Lovelace, Robin, and Morgane Dumont. 2016. *Spatial Microsimulation with R.* CRC Press. *http://bit.ly/spatialmicrosimR.*

McCallum, Ethan, and Stephen Weston. 2011. *Parallel R.* O'Reilly Media.

McConnell, Steve. 2004. *Code Complete.* Pearson Education.

Mersmann, Olaf. 2015. *Microbenchmark: Accurate Timing Functions.* *https://CRAN.R-project.org/package=microbenchmark.*

Peng, Roger. 2014. *R Programming for Data Science.* Leanpub. *https://leanpub.com/rprogramming.*

Pereira, Michelle Jessica, Brooke Kaye Coombes, Tracy Anne Comans, and Venerina Johnston. 2015. "The Impact of Onsite Workplace Health-Enhancing Physical Activity Interventions on Worker Productivity: A Systematic Review." *Occupational and Environmental Medicine* 72 (6). BMJ Publishing Group Ltd: 401–12.

PMBoK, A. 2000. "Guide to the Project Management Body of Knowledge." *Project Management Institute*, Pennsylvania USA.

R Core Team. 2016. "R Installation and Administration." *R Foundation for Statistical Computing. https://cran.r-project.org/doc/manuals/r-release/R-admin.html.*

Sanchez, Gaston. 2013. "Handling and Processing Strings in R." *Trowchez Editions. http://bit.ly/handlingstringsR.*

Sekhon, Jasjeet S. 2006. "The Art of Benchmarking: Evaluating the Performance of R on Linux and OS X." *The Political Methodologist* 14 (1): 15–19.

Spector, Phil. 2008. *Data Manipulation with R.* Springer Science & Business Media.

Sveidqvist, Knut, Mike Bostock, Chris Pettitt, Mike Daines, Andrei Kashcha, and Richard Iannone. 2016. *DiagrammeR: Create Graph Diagrams and Flowcharts Using R*. https://CRAN.R-project.org/package=DiagrammeR.

Visser, Marco D., Sean M. McMahon, Cory Merow, Philip M. Dixon, Sydne Record, and Eelke Jongejans. 2015. "Speeding Up Ecological and Evolutionary Computations in R; Essentials of High Performance Computing for Biologists." Edited by Francis Ouellette. PLOS Computational Biology 11 (3): e1004140. doi:10.1371/journal.pcbi. 1004140 (*http://bit.ly/speedingupeco*).

Wickham, Hadley. 2010. "Stringr: Modern, Consistent String Processing." *The R Journal* 2 (2): 38–40.

———. 2014a. *Advanced R*. CRC Press.

———. 2014b. "Tidy Data." *The Journal of Statistical Software* 14 (5).

———. 2015a. *Ggplot2movies: Movies Data*. https://CRAN.R-project.org/package=ggplot2movies.

———. 2015b. *Pryr: Tools for Computing on the Language*. https://CRAN.R-project.org/package=pryr.

———. 2015c. *R Packages*. O'Reilly Media.

———. 2016a. *Feather: R Bindings to the Feather 'API'*. https://CRAN.R-project.org/package=feather.

———. 2016b. *Tidyr: Easily Tidy Data with spread() and gather() Functions*. https://CRAN.R-project.org/package=tidyr.

Wickham, Hadley, and Winston Chang. 2016a. *Devtools: Tools to Make Developing R Packages Easier*. https://CRAN.R-project.org/package=devtools.

———. 2016b. *Ggplot2: An Implementation of the Grammar of Graphics*. https://CRAN.R-project.org/package=ggplot2.

Wickham, Hadley, and Romain Francois. 2016. *Dplyr: A Grammar of Data Manipulation*. https://CRAN.R-project.org/package=dplyr.

Wickham, Hadley, Romain Francois, and Kirill Müller. 2016. *Tibble: Simple Data Frames*. https://CRAN.R-project.org/package=tibble.

Wickham, Hadley, Jim Hester, and Romain Francois. 2016. *Readr: Read Tabular Data*. https://CRAN.R-project.org/package=readr.

Wickham, Hadley, David A. James, and Seth Falcon. 2014. *RSQLite: SQLite Interface for R*. https://CRAN.R-project.org/package=RSQLite.

Xie, Yihui. 2015. *Dynamic Documents with R and Knitr*. Vol. 29. CRC Press.

———. 2016a. *Bookdown: Authoring Books with R Markdown. https://CRAN.R-project.org/package=bookdown.*

———. 2016b. *FormatR: Format R Code Automatically. https://CRAN.R-project.org/package=formatR.*

———. 2016c. *Knitr: A General-Purpose Package for Dynamic Report Generation in R. https://CRAN.R-project.org/package=knitr.*

Zeileis, Achim, and the R community. 2016. *Fortunes: R Fortunes. https://CRAN.R-project.org/package=fortunes.*

Index

Symbols

&, && (AND operator), 134
.csv files, 88
.Rdata, 94
.Rds, 94
.Renviron file, 26, 33-34
    location of, 27
    storing passwords in, 120
.Rprofile, 26, 28-33, 31
    hidden environments with, 32
    location of, 27
    setting CRAN mirror, 30
    setting options, 30
    useful functions, 32
? prefix, 179
?? symbol, 177
|, || (OR operator), 134

A

aggregation (see data aggregation)
algorithmic efficiency, 4
AND (&, &&) operator, 134
anyNA() function, 135
apply function family, 57-61
    movies dataset example, 59
    parallel versions of, 140
    resources for, 60
    type consistency and, 60
apply() function, 57-61, 134
apropos(), 177
argument passing, assignment vs., 168
ASCII character set, 154
assertive.reflection package, 19
autocompletion, 39-40

B

base R
    converting factors to numerics, 134
    determining which indices are TRUE, 133
    if() vs. ifelse() functions, 131
    integer data type, 135
    is.na() and anyNA(), 135
    logical AND and OR, 134
    matrices, 135-137
    pattern matching with, 106
    reversing elements, 133
    row and column operations, 134
    sorting and ordering, 132
Basic Linear Algebra System (see BLAS)
benchmarking
    binary file formats, 94-96
    BLAS resources, 46
    for efficient programming, 9-11
benchmarkme package, 156, 161
binary file formats
    benchmarking, 94-96
    feather, 94
    for IO, 93-96
    Protocol Buffers for, 96
    Rds vs. Rdata, 94
BLAS framework, 43-46
    benchmarking resources, 46
    testing performance gains from, 44
braces, curly ({}), 169
branches, 172
broom package, 105
byte, 154

C

C++
  cppFunction() command, 144
  data types, 145
  R functions vs., 143
  Rcpp and, 143
  Rcpp sugar and, 149
  sourceCpp() function, 145
caching
  function closures, 63
  variables, 61-64
cat() function, 55
categorical variables, 56
central processing unit (CPU), 160
chaining, 112
cheat sheets, 182
chunking, 73
class, of columns, 110
clones, 172
closures, 63
cloud computing, 162
code profiling, 128-131
  efficiency and, 9, 11-14
  profvis, 129-131
code review, 173
coding style
  assigning objects to values, 168
  commenting, 166
  curly braces, 169
  filenames, 165
  for efficient collaboration, 164-169
  importance of consistency, 8
  indentation, 168
  loading packages, 166
  lubridate package example, 167
  object names, 167
  reformatting code with RStudio, 165
  spacing, 168
collaboration, 163-174
  code review, 173
  tips for, 164
  version control, 169-173
columns
  apply() function and, 134
  changing class, 110
  renaming, 110
comments/commenting, 166
commits, 170
compiler package, 64-67, 65

compiling code, 66
Comprehensive R Archive Network (see CRAN
  entries)
CPU (central processing unit), 160
CRAN (Comprehensive R Archive Network), 3
CRAN mirror, 30
csv files, 88
curly braces, 169

D

data aggregation, 114-116
data carpentry, 99-125
  combining datasets, 118-119
  data frames with tibble, 100
  data processing with data.table, 123-125
  databases and, 119-122
  dplyr for data processing, 108-113
  tidyr for, 102-107
  tips for, 100
data frames, 100
data input/output (see input/output (IO))
data processing, 108
  (see also data carpentry)
  data aggregation, 114-116
  data.table for, 123-125
  dplyr, 108-113
  nonstandard evaluation, 117
data tidying, 102-105
  gather(), 103
  regular expressions and, 106
  splitting joint variables with separate(), 104
  tidyr for, 102-107
data.table package, 123-125
databases
  data carpentry and, 119-122
  dplyr and, 121
datasets
  combining, 118-119
  for illustrating questions, 184
DBI, 120
deep learning, 185
dependencies, R packages with, 24
documentation, R Markdown for, 81
double-precision floating-point format, 135
dplyr
  chaining operations with, 112
  changing column classes, 110
  data aggregation, 114-116
  data processing with, 108-113

database access via, 121
filtering rows, 111
nonstandard evaluation, 117
renaming columns, 110
verb functions, 108
drat package, 181
dual in-line memory modules (DIMMs), 156
dynamic documentation, 81

E

EC2 (Elastic Compute Cloud), 162
efficiency
about, 4-6
benchmarking, 9-11
consistent code style/conventions, 8
cross-transferable skills for, 7-9
defined, 4
importance of, 6
in R programming, 4-6
of programmer, 7
profiling, 9, 11-14
touch typing, 7
ways in which R encourages/guides, 5
efficient package, 130, 178
Elastic Compute Cloud (EC2), 162

F

factors, 56
converting to numerics, 134
for fixed set of categories, 57
inherent order, 56
fatal errors, 53
feather (file format), 94
file paths, 28
file.path() function, 28
filenames, consistent style for, 165
filter() function, 111
forks, 172
fread() function
read_csv() vs., 90-92
speed of, 89
function calls
assignment operator vs. argument passing
operator, 168
library, 166
minimizing, 48
function closures, 63
functions, help pages for, 179-181
fuzzy matching, 118

G

gather() function, 103
Gentleman, Robert, 5
Git
about, 169
branches, 172
clones, 172
forks, 172
pull requests, 173
RStudio and, 170
GitHub, 171
graphics, factors for ordering in, 56

H

hard disc drive (HDD), 158
hardware, 153-162
bits and bytes, 154
cloud computing, 162
CPU, 160
hard drives, 158
operating systems, 159
RAM, 155-157
tips for, 153
HDD (hard disc drive), 158
help, R
functions, 179-181
Rs internal help, 176-182
searching for topics in, 177
source code, 181
swirl, 182
vignettes, 178
help.start() function, 3
helper functions, 32
hidden environments, 32

I

IDE (integrated development environment)
(see RStudio)
if() function, ifelse() function vs., 131
Ihaka, Ross, 5, 157
indentation, 168
indices, determining which are TRUE, 133
input/output (IO), 85-98
accessing data stored in packages, 97
binary file formats, 93-96
data from internet, 96
plain-text formats, 88-93
rio, 86-87

tips for, 86
installation
    R, 22
    R packages, 14, 23
    R packages with dependencies, 24
integer data type, 135
integrated development environment (IDE)
    (see RStudio)
internal help, R, 176-182
International System of Units (SI) prefixes, 154
internet, data from, 96
interpreters, 45
invisible() function, 55
IO (see input/output)
is.na() function, 135

J

joining, 118-119
joining variable, 118

K

keyboard shortcuts, 36, 40
Knuth, Donald, 127

L

lapply() function, 59
learning, 175-187
    asking questions efficiently, 184
    in depth, 185
    online resources, 3, 182-184
    Rs internal help for, 3, 176-182
    Stack Overflow site, 183
    teaching, 187
    tips for, 175
library function calls, 166
Linux
    C++ compiler, 128
    parallel code under, 141
    R installation, 22
    system monitoring on, 20
loops, Rcpp and, 146-149
lubridate package, 167

M

Mac OS
    C++ compiler installation, 128
    R installation, 22
    R updates, 23

system monitoring on, 20
mailing lists, 184
matrices, 135-137
    integer data type, 135
    sparse, 137
memoise package, 62
memory allocation, 49
merging, 118-119
message() function, 55
METACRAN, 80
microbenchmark package, 9
Microsoft R Open, 45
missing values, 135
MonetDB, 120
Monopoly (game), 138
Monte Carlo simulation
    code profiling, 130
    parallel computing for, 140
    vectorized code, 51
MRAN, 80

N

non-standard evaluation (NSE), 64, 117
normalizePath() function, 28
noSQL, 120

O

object display, 41
objects
    assigning to values, 168
    naming of, 167
online learning resources, 182-184, 184
    mailing lists, 184
    R-bloggers, 183
    Stack Overflow, 183
operating system (OS)
    32-bit vs. 64-bit, 159
    R setup, 18-21
    resource monitoring and, 19-21
optim() function, 179-181
optimization, 127-151
    code profiling, 128-131
    efficient base R, 131-138
    movie_square() function, 138
    parallel computing, 139-142
    Rcpp, 142-151
    tips for, 128
options() function, 30
OR (|, ||) operator, 134

Oracle, R-interpreter, 46
ordering, 56, 133
OS (see operating system)
OS X, parallel code under, 141

P

packages
    loading, 166
        (see also .Renviron file)
    R (see R packages)
panes, RStudio layout, 36-38
parallel computing, 139-142
    apply functions, 140
    exit functions, 141
    Snakes and Ladders simulation, 140
    under Linux or OS X, 141
parallel package, 139, 140
passwords, storing in .Renviron, 120
pathological package, 28
plain-text data files
    fread() vs. read_csv(), 90-92
    I/O with, 88-93
    limitations to, 93
    preprocessing text outside R, 92
pointer object, 145
pqrR, 45
profiling (see code profiling)
profvis, 129-131
    basics, 129
    Monopoly simulation example, 130
programmer productivity/efficiency, 4
    (see also workflow)
programming, 47-67
    apply function family, 57-61
    byte compiler, 64-67
    caching variables, 61-64
    communicating with user, 53-56
    factors, 56
    general advice, 48-53
    memory allocation, 49
    tips for, 47
    vectorized code, 50-53
project management
    chunking, 73
    RStudio, 41
    SMART criteria for objectives, 74
    visualizing plans with R, 75
project planning
    package selection, 76-80

project management and, 72-76
    typology, 70-72
    visualizing plans with R, 75
Protocol Buffers
    binary data storage with, 96
pryr package, 155
publication, 80-84
    R Markdown framework for documenta-
        tion, 81
    treating projects as R packages, 83
pull request (PR), 173

Q

questions
    asking efficiently, 184
    avoiding redundant, 183
    minimal dataset for illustrating, 184
    minimal example for illustrating, 185

R

R
    C++ functions vs., 143
    installing, 22
    updating, 23
R Markdown, 81
R package ecosystem, 78
R packages
    accessing data stored in, 97
    installation, 14, 23
    installation with dependencies, 24
    searching for, 78
    selection as part of planning process, 76-80
    selection criteria, 78
    treating projects as, 42, 83
    updating, 24
R startup, 25-35
    arguments, 25
    location of startup files, 27-28
R-bloggers, 183
R-project website, 182
random access memory (RAM), 155-157
Rcpp, 142-151
    C++ data types, 145
    C++ functions, 143
    cppFunction() command, 144
    matrices, 149
    resources/documentation, 150
    sourceCpp() function, 145
    sugar, 149

vectors and loops, 146-149
Rdata, 94
Rds, 94
read.csv() function, 89
readr package, 86, 88-92
read_csv() function
    factors and, 57
    fread() vs., 90-92
    speed of, 89
reformatting, 165
regular expressions, 106
rename() function, 110
Renjin, 46
Renviron file, 26, 33-34
    location of, 27
    storing passwords in, 120
resource monitoring, 19-21
rev() function, 133
Rho, 45
rio package, 86-87
RODBC, 120
rows, filtering with dplyr, 111
Rprof() function, 128
Rprofile, 26, 28-33, 31
    hidden environments with, 32
    location of, 27
    setting CRAN mirror, 30
    setting options, 30
    useful functions, 32
RStudio
    autocompletion, 39-40
    Git integration in, 170
    installing and updating, 35
    keyboard shortcuts, 36, 40
    object display and output table, 41
    options, 38
    project management, 41
    R package updates, 25
    reformatting code with, 165
    setup, 35-43
    window pane layout, 36-38
RStudio mirror, 30

S

separate() function, 104
setup, 17-46
    alternative R interpreters, 45
    BLAS framework, 43-46
    installing R, 22

operating system, 18-21
R package installation, 23
R startup, 25-35
R version, 21-25
RStudio, 35-43
tips for, 18
updating R, 23
updating R packages, 24
shared memory systems (see parallel computing)
shortcuts, keyboard, 36, 40
SI (International System of Units) prefixes, 154
SMART criteria, 74
solid state drive (SSD), 159
sorting, 132
source code, reading, 181
sourceCpp() function, 145
spacing, 168
sparse matrices, 137
SSD (solid state drive), 159
Stack Overflow (programming help site), 183
startup files, R, 26-34
    .Renviron, 33-34
    .Rprofile, 28-33
    location of, 27-28
startup, R, 25-35
stop() function, 53
stream processing, 92
stringr, pattern matching with, 106
style (see coding style)
subsetting, 123, 136
sugar, 149
swirl, 182
Sys.getenv() function, 33
system variables (see .Renviron file)

T

tables, gather() function and, 103
tbl_df data frame class, 100
teaching, as form of learning, 187
technical debt, 72
TERR, 46
tibble, 100
Tibco, 46
tidy data, 103
tidyr package, 102-105
    data tidying with, 102-105
    splitting joint variables with separate(), 104
    various functions, 105

touch typing, 7

U

Ubuntu
    R packages with dependencies, 24
    R updates, 23
updating
    R, 23
    R packages, 24
user, communicating with, 53-56
    fatal errors, 53
    informative output, 55
    invisible returns, 55
    warnings, 54

V

values, assigning objects to, 168
variables, caching, 61-64
vector
    determining which indices are TRUE, 133
    matrices and, 149
    pre-allocating, 49
    Rcpp and, 146-149
    sorting, 132
vectorized code
    efficient programming and, 50-53
    Monte Carlo integration, 51
version control, 169-173
    branches, 172
    clones, 172
    commits, 170

    forks, 172
    Git integration in RStudio, 170
    GitHub, 171
    pull requests, 173
vignette() function, 3
vignettes, finding/using, 3, 178

W

warning() function, 54
wide boundary search, 177
wide data, 102
window panes, in RStudio layout, 36-38
Windows
    C++ compiler installation, 128
    file paths in R, 28
    R installation, 22
    R packages with dependencies, 24
    R updates, 23
    system monitoring on, 20
workflow, 69-84
    chunking, 73
    defined, 69
    package selection, 76-80
    project management and, 72-76
    project planning typology, 70-72
    publication, 80-84
    RStudio, 41
    SMART criteria for objectives, 74
    tips for, 70
    typology, 70-72
    visualizing plans with R, 75

About the Authors

Colin Gillespie (*http://www.mas.ncl.ac.uk/~ncsg3/*) is senior lecturer (associate professor) at Newcastle University, UK. His research interests are high-performance statistical computing and Bayesian statistics. He is regularly employed as a consultant by Jumping Rivers (*http://www.jumpingrivers.com/*) and has been teaching R since 2005 at a variety of levels, ranging from beginners to advanced programming.

Robin Lovelace (*http://robinlovelace.net*) is a researcher at the Leeds Institute for Transport Studies (ITS) (*http://www.its.leeds.ac.uk/*) and the Leeds Institute for Data Analytics (LIDA) (*http://lida.leeds.ac.uk/about-lida/contact/*). Robin has many years using R for academic research and has taught numerous R courses at all levels. He has developed a number of popular R resources, including Introduction to Visualising Spatial Data in R (*https://github.com/Robinlovelace/Creating-maps-in-R*) and *Spatial Microsimulation with R* (*https://github.com/Robinlovelace/spatial-microsim-book*) (Lovelace and Dumont 2016). These skills have been applied on a number of projects with real-world applications, including the Propensity to Cycle Tool (*http://www.pct.bike/*), a nationally scalable interactive online mapping application, and the **stplanr** (*https://github.com/ropensci/stplanr*) package.

Colophon

The animal on the cover of *Efficient R Programming* is the grey heron (*Ardea cinerea*). Grey herons are large wading birds, measuring up to 100 cm in height with a nearly 200 cm wingspan. They are long-legged, which lets them easily wade in the shallows of their native wetland habitat. They hunt fish, amphibians, small mammals, and insects by standing motionless in shallow water throughout the day, then striking unsuspecting prey with their long bill. At night, they roost in trees or on cliffs, where they also lay eggs and raise their young.

Grey herons can be found throughout Europe, Asia, and Africa. Most gray herons live in the same region year round, but those living in colder northern regions migrate south for the winter. They are mostly grey in color, with a white neck and black streaks on the head and wings.

Grey herons have been a part of several ancient mythological systems. During the New Kingdom period in Egypt, the deity Bennu, god of the sun, creation, and rebirth, was represented as a grey heron. In pre-Christian Rome, the gray heron was a symbol of divinination used by priests to predict the future.

Many of the animals on O'Reilly covers are endangered; all of them are important to the world. To learn more about how you can help, go to *animals.oreilly.com*.

The cover image is from *Meyers Kleines Lexicon*. The cover fonts are URW Typewriter and Guardian Sans. The text font is Adobe Minion Pro; the heading font is Adobe Myriad Condensed; and the code font is Dalton Maag's Ubuntu Mono.

Get even more for your money.

Join the O'Reilly Community, and register the O'Reilly books you own. It's free, and you'll get:

- $4.99 ebook upgrade offer
- 40% upgrade offer on O'Reilly print books
- Membership discounts on books and events
- Free lifetime updates to ebooks and videos
- Multiple ebook formats, DRM FREE
- Participation in the O'Reilly community
- Newsletters
- Account management
- 100% Satisfaction Guarantee

Signing up is easy:

1. Go to: oreilly.com/go/register
2. Create an O'Reilly login.
3. Provide your address.
4. Register your books.

Note: English-language books only

To order books online:
oreilly.com/store

For questions about products or an order:
orders@oreilly.com

To sign up to get topic-specific email announcements and/or news about upcoming books, conferences, special offers, and new technologies:
elists@oreilly.com

For technical questions about book content:
booktech@oreilly.com

To submit new book proposals to our editors:
proposals@oreilly.com

O'Reilly books are available in multiple DRM-free ebook formats. For more information:
oreilly.com/ebooks

Learn from experts.
Find the answers you need.

Sign up for a **10-day free trial** to get **unlimited access** to all of the content on Safari, including Learning Paths, interactive tutorials, and curated playlists that draw from thousands of ebooks and training videos on a wide range of topics, including data, design, DevOps, management, business—and much more.

Start your free trial at:
oreilly.com/safari

(No credit card required.)

Milton Keynes UK
Ingram Content Group UK Ltd.
UKHW012003050824
446577UK00007B/158